The Virgin Suicides

Based on the best-selling novel by Jeffrey Eugenides, *The Virgin Suicides* is director Sofia Coppola's evocative debut feature of young love, sex, loss and family pressures in mid-1970s America. Acclaimed by both critics and audiences on release, the film is now viewed as a remarkable and bold feature by a significant female director addressing many issues related to youth, female sexuality and family.

This book helps readers understand the film's significance and the stylistic and storytelling choices made by director Coppola. The analysis of the film occurs around three interlocking arguments: the unusual structuring absence in the film, the intricate manner through which music is used in the drama, communication and character creation, and the film's careful and specific referencing of advertising in the 1970s (the decade of the film's narrative). The film's enigmatic structure and unique storytelling devices and their relationship to female adolescence, sexuality and ideology are also considered in depth. Without solving the mysteries of the film, the book is designed to uncover the reasons why the film continues to fascinate viewers so many years after its release.

Justin Wyatt is Associate Director of the Harrington School of Communication and Media at the University of Rhode Island. He teaches in Communication Studies and Film/Media. He is the author of *High Concept: Movies and Marketing in Hollywood* and co-editor of *Contemporary American Independent Film: From the Margins to the Mainstream*.

Cinema and Youth Cultures
Series Editors: Siân Lincoln & Yannis Tzioumakis

Cinema and Youth Cultures engages with well-known youth films from American cinema as well as the cinemas of other countries. Using a variety of methodological and critical approaches the series volumes provide informed accounts of how young people have been represented in film, while also exploring the ways in which young people engage with films made for and about them. In doing this, the Cinema and Youth Cultures series contributes to important and long-standing debates about youth cultures, how these are mobilized and articulated in influential film texts and the impact that these texts have had on popular culture at large.

Grease
Barbara Jane Brickman

Boyhood
Timothy Shary

Easy A
Betty Kaklamanidou

The Hunger Games
Catherine Driscoll and Alexandra Heatwole

L'Auberge Espagnole
Ben McCann

The Virgin Suicides
Justin Wyatt

For more information about this series, please visit: www.routledge.com/Cinema-and-Youth-Cultures/book-series/CYC

The Virgin Suicides

Reverie, Sorrow and Young Love

Justin Wyatt

Taylor & Francis Group

LONDON AND NEW YORK

First published 2019
by Routledge

2 Park Square, Milton Park, Abingdon, Oxfordshire OX14 4RN
52 Vanderbilt Avenue, New York, NY 10017

Routledge is an imprint of the Taylor & Francis Group, an informa business

First issued in paperback 2020

Library of Congress Cataloging-in-Publication Data
Names: Wyatt, Justin, 1963– author.
Title: The virgin suicides : reverie, sorrow and young love /
    Justin Wyatt.
Description: London ; New York : Routledge, 2018. | Series:
    Cinema and youth cultures ; 7 | Includes bibliographical
    references and index.
Identifiers: LCCN 2018018193 | ISBN 9781138046443 (hardback :
    alk. paper) | ISBN 9781315171395 (ebook : alk. paper)
Subjects: LCSH: Virgin suicides (Motion picture) | Youth in
    motion pictures.
Classification: LCC PN1997.V4974 W94 2018 | DDC
    791.43/72—dc23
LC record available at https://lccn.loc.gov/2018018193

ISBN: 978-1-138-04644-3 (hbk)
ISBN: 978-0-367-60692-3 (pbk)

Typeset in Times New Roman
by Apex CoVantage, LLC

For Janet Bergstrom and Jeffrey Clarke,
with respect and love

Contents

Figures

Series Editors' Introduction

Despite the high visibility of youth films in the global media marketplace, especially since the 1980s when Conglomerate Hollywood realized that such films were not only strong box office performers but also the starting point for ancillary sales in other media markets as well as for franchise building, academic studies that focused specifically on such films were slow to materialize. Arguably the most important factor behind academia's reluctance to engage with youth films was a (then) widespread perception within the Film and Media Studies communities that such films held little cultural value and significance, and therefore were not worthy of serious scholarly research and examination. Just like the young subjects they represented, whose interests and cultural practices have been routinely deemed transitional and transitory, so were the films that represented them perceived as fleeting and easily digestible, destined to be forgotten quickly, as soon as the next youth film arrived on cinema screens a week later.

Under these circumstances, and despite a small number of pioneering studies in the 1980s and early 1990s, the field of 'youth film studies' did not really start blossoming and attracting significant scholarly attention until the 2000s and in combination with similar developments in cognate areas such as 'girl studies.' However, because of the paucity of material in the previous decades, the majority of these new studies in the 2000s focused primarily on charting the field and therefore steered clear of long, in-depth examinations of youth films or was exemplified by edited collections that chose particular films to highlight certain issues to the detriment of others. In other words, despite providing often wonderfully rich accounts of youth cultures as these have been captured by key films, these studies could not have possibly dedicated sufficient space to engage with more than just a few key aspects of youth films.

In more recent (post-2010) years a number of academic studies started delimiting their focus and therefore providing more space for in-depth examinations of key types of youth films, such as slasher films and biker films or examining youth films in particular historical periods. From that point on, it was a matter of time for the first publications that focused exclusively on key youth films from a number of perspectives to appear (*Mamma Mia! The Movie*, *Twilight* and *Dirty Dancing* are among the first films to receive this treatment). Conceived primarily as edited collections, these studies provided a multifaceted analysis of these films, focusing on such issues as the politics of representing youth, the stylistic and narrative choices that characterize these films and the extent to which they are representative of a youth cinema, the ways these films address their audiences, the ways youth audiences engage with these films, the films' industrial location and other relevant issues.

It is within this increasingly maturing and expanding academic environment that the **Cinema and Youth Cultures** volumes arrive, aiming to consolidate existing knowledge, provide new perspectives, apply innovative methodological approaches, offer sustained and in-depth analyses of key films and therefore become the 'go to' resource for students and scholars interested in theoretically informed, authoritative accounts of youth cultures in film. As editors, we have tried to be as inclusive as possible in our selection of key examples of youth films by commissioning volumes on films that span the history of cinema, including the silent film era; that portray contemporary youth cultures as well as ones associated with particular historical periods; that represent examples of mainstream and independent cinema; that originate in American cinema and the cinemas of other nations; that attracted significant critical attention and commercial success during their initial release and that were 'rediscovered' after an unpromising initial critical reception. Together these volumes are going to advance youth film studies while also being able to offer extremely detailed examinations of films that are now considered significant contributions to cinema and our cultural life more broadly.

We hope readers will enjoy the series.

Siân Lincoln & Yannis Tzioumakis
Cinema & Youth Cultures Series Editors

Acknowledgments

I am indebted to the series editors, Yannis Tzioumakis and Siân Lincoln, for inviting me to contribute to their book series. As editors, they have been remarkable in terms of support and clear judgment to move the book forward in the most productive direction. The fact that they are also such open, collaborative and friendly mentors has made the journey even more enjoyable.

At the University of Rhode Island, I am blessed to have the support of Associate Dean Adam Roth, Dean Jen Riley, and Film/Media Program Chair Rebecca Romanow. All have aided considerably in my ability to focus on this project and to explore an array of issues from the book in my courses. Colleagues and friends from the University of Rhode Island have made my trip back to academia a very pleasant one. In my 'third career,' I have been welcomed and bolstered by many at URI: Steve Wood, Mary Healey Jamiel, Mary Cappello, Jean Walton, Tom Zorabedian, Marybeth Reilly-McGovern, Keith Brown, Hollie Smith, Ian Reyes, Kathleen Torrens, Winnie Brownell, Kevin McClure, Rachel DiCioccio, Bob Schwegler, Ashish Chadha, Lynne Derbyshire, David Elperin, and Adam David Roth.

Fred Fuchs and Jane Findlay Clarke were helpful in discussing the film with me. As Executive Producer, Fred's perspective was particularly useful in understanding the larger context of the film.

Finally, friends, near and far, have stuck by me during my transition back to academia and scholarship: Douglas Hodapp, Doug Cunningham, Kathleen McHugh, Patrice Petro, Sharon Hodapp, Irene Manahan, Audrey Fang Koch, Leslie LeMond, Chris Holmlund, Jon Lewis, Tim Anderson, Bobbie Leflein, Christina Clarke Dewar, Alisa Perren, Kevin Sanson, Phoebe Roth, Tom Schatz, Matthew Bernstein, and Gilberto Blasini. I am grateful for all of you, and so many more.

Introduction

Published in 1993, Jeffrey Eugenides' *The Virgin Suicides* was lauded for offering a powerful tale of loss in a middle class Michigan family in the mid-1970s. Eugenides was praised for his careful observation and detail evoking both the fascination—and horror—of teenage sexuality and the connection between love, obsession and madness. As author Jay McInerney commented on the book, 'Jeffrey Eugenides has created a mythology out of the ostensible common materials of middle class, middle-American life . . . purveying a kind of domestic magic realism which is all his own' (in Eugenides 1993: no page). Sofia Coppola was so taken with the novel that she drafted a screenplay without, in fact, owning the rights. On completion, she was able to convince the rights-holders to work together so that she could craft her debut film (Smaill 2013: 154). Coppola's film was presented to strong critical acclaim in the Director's Fortnight at the Cannes Film Festival in 1999. After a bidding war for the distribution rights took place at Cannes, the US release was sponsored by Paramount Classics, the 'art house' arm of Paramount Pictures in May 2000. Critically acclaimed, the film posted solid art house grosses both domestically and internationally.[1]

Mirroring Eugenides' book closely, Coppola's film concerns the Lisbon family: a high school math teacher (James Woods), his solemn and religious wife (Kathleen Turner), and their five daughters, ranging in age from 13 to 17. Taking place in a quiet suburban neighborhood in mid-1970s Michigan, the story begins with the attempted suicide of Cecilia (Hanna Hall), the youngest daughter. When chastised by her doctor for not even knowing what life is like at that age, Cecilia responds coolly with 'Obviously, doctor, you have never been a 13-year-old girl.' Encouraged to offer more social outlets for Cecilia, the parents plan an innocuous basement party at the Lisbon home. The event is cut short when Cecilia jumps from her bedroom window and is impaled on the fence in the front yard. After this point, the family is 'tainted' within the neighborhood, with people gossiping about the suicide, the reasons behind it, and the family dynamics at play. After a group date goes south when the most rebellious girl, Lux (Kirsten Dunst), stays out all night with her dashing prom date, Trip Fontaine (Josh Hartnett), the Lisbon parents pull the girls from school. In their isolation, the girls start a fractured communication with the local male teenagers in the neighborhood through postcards and playing pop songs to each other over the phone. One night the girls summon the boys to come to the Lisbon home after the parents have gone to sleep. As events unfold, the surprise for the boys is one of tragedy and self-violence ultimately rather than romance and escape.

This book seeks to enhance understanding of the film through tracing key contextual elements and influences on the project. The first two chapters situate *The Virgin Suicides* as part of a larger institutional framework. In the first chapter, I place Sofia Coppola's debut in the context of female independent filmmaking of the 1990s. While the explosion of independent cinema in that decade was buttressed by an array of different, previously marginalized voices, there were still relatively few women directors operating either inside or outside the independent film world. The first half of the decade evidenced isolated instances of female directors making an impact, such as Julie Dash's *Daughters of the Dust* (1991), Allison Anders' *Gas Food Lodging* (1992) and Leslie Harris' *Just another Girl on the I.R.T.* (1992). While all these films are an important part of the indie film movement, three films by female directors extend the ways in which genre, female sexuality, and transgression were engaged: Jennifer Montgomery's *Art for Teachers of Children* (1995), Kelly Reichardt's *River of Grass* (1995), and Lisa Krueger's *Manny & Lo* (1996). These three films present a space for female sexuality that is uncompromised, yet troubling in its engagement with the dominant ideology. Unlike traditional Hollywood storytelling, the female characters cannot be reduced to simple motivations or placed within the confines of genre storytelling. These films 'set the stage' for *The Virgin Suicides* through offering female protagonists whose sexuality defies social parameters and the expectations for an audience. Through tracing these films' presentation of the female characters, their sexuality, and the ways through which their sexuality poses a threat to social norms, the thematic concerns and stylistic experimentation in *The Virgin Suicides* will be seen as continuing the dialog started by earlier female directors in the mid-1990s.

The second chapter addresses the other key determinant of *The Virgin Suicides*, the production company American Zoetrope and the family Coppola. Now co-owned by Sofia and her brother Roman Coppola, American Zoetrope began life for father Francis Coppola as Zoetrope Studios in 1969. As part of the 'next generation' of Coppolas, Sofia was able to utilize the structure, organization and creative talent of American Zoetrope for her debut feature. The other way that American Zoetrope influenced *The Virgin Suicides* is through the Coppola lineage. Patriarch Francis continually created opportunities for Sofia to experiment creatively while growing up, from acting in *Rumble Fish* (1983) and *The Godfather Part III* (1990) to co-writing the script for his segment 'Life Without Zoe' in *New York Stories* (1989). Some may interpret these efforts as nothing more than exploitation, particularly casting Sofia as a last minute replacement for Winona Ryder in *The Godfather Part III*. Regardless of the motives, these efforts did, in fact, create a space for expression in a public way for Sofia. The strain throughout much of these efforts, including *The Virgin Suicides*, is loss, which might even be considered a structuring absence. The origins of this theme are unknown, although the death of Sofia's brother Gian-Carlo (Gio) at age 23 in a tragic 1986 boating accident may be linked thematically. Echoes of personal loss are reflected in many of the Coppola projects after that date: Sofia's 'Life Without Zoe' in which a young girl living by herself tries to reconcile her estranged parents; mother Eleanor's memoir *Notes on a Life* detailing each day after the death of Gio; Roman's own American Zoetrope debut feature *CQ* (2000) offering a hero adrift abroad, separated from his family and facing creative bankruptcy. Sofia Coppola's *The Virgin Suicides* links to this theme in the family Coppola response to the tragic loss of Gio. Both center on the loss of a young life, its impact on a family, and the surrounding public inquiry/curiosity around the event. Further, *The Virgin Suicides* is definitely situated as a memorial, narrated by one of the neighborhood boys now twenty-five years after the tragedy. For Coppola, the creative act of making *The Virgin Suicides* is memorializing also, sifting through the loss of a sibling and attempting to reclaim their role and presence in the family.

The third chapter of my book takes a more direct entry point to the film. I am interested in exploring the primary enigma: why do the Lisbon girls commit mass suicide? To unpack this question, Coppola's narrational techniques and devices must be identified and analyzed. At the most global level, the film is structured around a middle-aged male's recollection of the events leading up to the suicides. Although the strong suggestion is that one of the neighborhood teenage boys, all grown up, is the narrator, Coppola leaves the exact identification of the narrator ambiguous (it should be noted that Eugenides' novel is structured around multiple male narrators, supposedly the group of neighborhood boys grown, rather than a single voice). The film begins with the narrator positioning the distance between events (twenty-five years) and recalling the group's continued fascination with the Lisbon suicides. As a result, the narrative of the film is setup as a chronology of events leading up to the suicides. Crucially, the viewer has access to these events through the narrator and his memory of events twenty-five years old. The result is an unreliable narrator. Some events are clearly aligned with the perspective of the neighborhood boys, others, however, are impossible for the narrator to know. Still other events are tonally so out of line with the general narrative trajectory that an audience member might wonder why they are included. This leaves the audience wondering if these curious events are either the imagination of the narrator or some kind of omniscient voice used to 'fill in' events as needed.

So *The Virgin Suicides* is structured not just around the single enigma, but rather the question: who is telling the story? The narration is, at times, contradictory and unreliable, confounding any simple way to interpret the events and understand the mystery of the Lisbon girls and their fate. This choice of narration mirrors the ways in which adolescents construct narrative events, allowing room for revision and foregoing many of the 'rules' of adult storytelling. The distant (in time and space) narrator at least helps to explain one of the other aspects of the film: the incomplete picture of psychological or dramatic explanation for the girls. For a film that starts with Cecilia's interview with a hospital psychiatrist, *The Virgin Suicides* actually eschews conventional psychological explanation for the girls and their action. This strategy makes the film a very interesting case for examining youth culture and the ways in which identity and psychology are presented in adolescents. The film's unusual exploration of youth, psychology and identity is manifested in several ways. Most obviously the narrator focuses his story primarily on two sisters, Cecilia and Lux, leaving the other three (Mary, Therese, Bonnie) undifferentiated and without any significant control of the development of the story. Since the story unfolds with three of its lead characters undefined, the mystery becomes even more difficult to uncover. With the male narrator as our guide, the viewer is literally within the male gaze—objectifying the sisters, compelled by their bond, and ignorant of their motives.

The viewer is left with a mystery in which the clues never completely, or even partially, explain the enigma at the center. From the perspective of the neighborhood boys, the mystery becomes how to understand female sexuality, and, by extension, the young female psyche. As such, this model reflects young people's characteristic narrational agency more generally through emphasizing these incomplete and partial representations of others. By the end of the film, the narrator is left adrift, recounting the incidents leading to the mass suicide, but uncovering only isolated incidents, brief notes and third-party memories of the Lisbon family. The chapter closes through drawing these parallels, and through suggesting how *The Virgin Suicides'* structure around an enigma offers a challenge to viewer expectations and conventional, linear storytelling.

Critic A.O. Scott commented in his *New York Times* review of the film, 'More than most recent movies about suburban adolescence, *The Virgin Suicides* catches both the triviality and the grandeur of youth, its prosaic details and its mythopoetic flights' (Scott 2000). The fourth chapter considers an important application of Scott's analysis, the use of music as part of a 'mythopoetic flight' and as a storytelling device. Music has been central to youth films for decades, with multiple examples illustrating how music, communication and identity formation are intricately connected. Coppola explores how music defines the adolescent individual and the group throughout *The Virgin Suicides*. Continually, music is used to help construct identity and to facilitate communication where otherwise there would be none for these young people.

Coppola cleverly uses music to evoke the mid-1970s era of singer-songwriter and soft pop albums and to suggest a contemporary perspective on the times through the soundtrack. Coppola commissioned the French electronic duo Air (Jean-Benoit Dunckel and Nicolas Godin) to construct the soundtrack. Their 1998 debut album, *Moon Safari*, was heavily indebted to aspects of the 1970s 'analog sound' through Moog synthesizers and valve amplifiers. Crucially, the 'chilled out' essence of the music is not a camp exercise. The duo earnestly places themes of love, loss and memory through the tracks rather than looking for a camp treatment from a music type popular twenty-five years earlier. The Air soundtrack to *The Virgin Suicides* follows directly from *Moon Safari*. Anchored by the single 'Playground Love,' the soundtrack is essentially variations on the themes of young love, memory and loss, all played out in lush synthesized tones more appropriate to 1975 than to the late 1990s. The chapter explores the specific instances of Air's music in relation to the narrative and mise-en-scène, arguing that the Air soundtrack is a key element to the creation of meaning.

The Virgin Suicides can be read as a film about missed communication or the impossibility to communicate effectively. Within the realm of psychotherapy and communication studies, there is a considerable literature on the difficulties of adolescent communication with peers, siblings, teachers and adults.[2] So many scenes in *The Virgin Suicides* are cued to female vs. male exchanges and are either misinterpreted or ignored. When the primary function of the music in the film's storytelling is not to comment on teen identity, it is specific and relates to the missed communication so important to the film. After they are in 'lock down,' forced to stay at home, even to the extent of missing school, the sisters try to connect to the neighborhood boys. Challenged, and somewhat intimidated, by the invitation from the girls, the teen boys respond by calling the Lisbon sisters' phone. Instead of talking, the boys just play a song, in its entirety, holding the phone to the record player, and then just hanging up. The girls follow suit, calling, playing a song and hanging up. Instead of building a real connection between the sisters and the teen boys, the groups substitute a curious pop culture referencing system. As Tim Anderson describes it (2013: 73), records are used as 'emotional ciphers' through which the adolescents communicate in *The Virgin Suicides*. In the process, though, Coppola makes the viewer to reconsider these songs in the context of the dramatic action. The chapter proceeds with a close analysis of the songs used by Coppola, their function in the storytelling, and the ways through which they morph the narrative and reflect on the larger experience of adolescent life.

While sexuality and sexual difference and the ways they are posed in the film are, directly or indirectly, the main focal points of the book in the first four chapters, the fifth chapter turns to this issue through a very particular lens of advertising. The chapter ties mass market advertising, print and television commercials, to the visual representations and style within the film. Coppola develops these very striking and memorable visual 'bursts' of the sisters. These are sometimes presented as the imaginings or reveries of the male teens as they consider the Lisbon sisters: Lux doing a hula dance, Lux dancing in a field with a unicorn in split screen, Cecilia dressed as an Indian princess, Bonnie blowing on a dandelion, and the final dream of all the sisters and male teens together in the station wagon, cruising down the freeway with the windows open and teens hugging each other. We are seeing these shots and scenes from the narrator's point-of-view, but, keep in mind, that the narrator is now a middle-aged man recalling events from his teenage years. The most powerful way to understand these reveries is not as elements of the narrative or as dreams, but rather as filtered experiences soaked in the world of mass media advertising of the 1970s. Coppola is channeling these fantasy images from an array of cosmetics, fashion and health ads of the decade. Interestingly, Coppola has continued these reveries in her marketing and advertising work: her 2013 commercial for the perfume Daisy by Marc Jacobs is shot in just the same style as these moments in *The Virgin Suicides*. My analysis will link these reveries to the print/TV ads of the period, showing a very similar ideology related to the family and female teens.

The book's concluding chapter places the themes, stylistic devices, and authorial traits in the context of Sofia Coppola's later work. Considering *The Virgin Suicides* against these later works, it is clear that the thematic concerns of dislocation, loss and the fragility of youth are revisited and deepened for Coppola.

The film is the first example of Coppola's focus on identity formation in adolescents and young adults. Issues with establishing or enacting a stable identity recur in the subsequent Coppola films, such as *Marie Antoinette* (2006) and *The Bling Ring* (2013), whether in teens or young adults. In addition, the patterned use of music and pop culture referencing so important to *The Virgin Suicides* also are crucial to all these other works. While *The Virgin Suicides* is a very faithful adaptation of Eugenides' novel, the film has an openness to allow Coppola to establish the narrational and thematic traits that have become characteristic of her as a film artist.

Over the course of her two-decade filmmaking career, Coppola has drawn considerable attention for her incisive portrayal of youth and adolescence. In 2017, Focus Features' online article, '7 Must-Haves for a Quintessential Sofia Coppola Film' makes this tendency explicit by identifying 'rites of passage' as a key element in the Coppola films: 'In nearly all of Coppola's films, young women discover who they are in wondrous way' (Anon 2017). Coppola agrees with this sentiment, claiming that 'I always like characters who are in the midst of a transition and trying to find their place in the world and their identity' (Gevinson 2013). The testament to Coppola's effectiveness in speaking to young women addressing life changes is evident through many posts online. Consider, for instance, two parallel online articles praising Coppola for her ability to understand young women: 'What Sofia Coppola's Films Taught Me about Being a Teenage Girl' and the similar, but more specific, 'What *Marie Antoinette* Taught Me about Being a Teenage Girl' (Ewens 2016). Both pieces identify the care with which Coppola is able to confront the fears of female adolescence, such as feeling trapped and despairing, but also the 'capricious, electrifying power of youth' (Woodhead 2017). Sofia Coppola's insight on the journey from girlhood to womanhood clearly has resonance for the young. This path began with her debut, a film that is centered on youth culture in the context of personal trauma and tragedy.

Notes

1. In fact, the film's foreign gross ($5.5 million) outstripped US domestic gross ($4.9 million); www.boxofficemojo.com/movies/?id=virginesuicides.html.
2. Consider, for instance, Adams et al. (1992), Cote (2000), and Cote and Levine (2016).

1 1990s Indie Cinema and the Path to *The Virgin Suicides*

The Virgin Suicides exists in a liminal space between the independent and the mainstream studio worlds. Distributed by a studio art house arm (Paramount Classics), based on a best-selling novel and featuring a well-known supporting cast, the film nevertheless engages with a subject matter that is both defiantly uncommercial and disturbing in nature. Despite this 'in between' status, I would argue that the aesthetic roots of *The Virgin Suicides* are, in fact, tied in several key ways to independent cinema of that decade. Completed in 1999, Sofia Coppola's *The Virgin Suicides* follows in the aesthetic and commercial trajectory of 'indie cinema' of the 1990s. In fact, the institutional connection to the independent film world has been a key theme throughout Coppola's career. With the exception of Columbia releasing *Marie Antoinette* (2006), all of Coppola's films have been released by distributors associated with independent cinema (Focus Features for *Lost in Translation* (2003), *Somewhere* (2010), and *The Beguiled* (2017); A24 for *The Bling Ring* (2013)). To understand the thematics and aesthetics of *The Virgin Suicides* fully, the context of 1990s independent cinema needs to be sketched. In particular, the contributions of 1990s female directors and their presentation of sexuality, kinship and female agency offer a path for Coppola's vision in her short film *Lick the Star* (1998) and in her first feature. While Coppola's debut marks an extraordinary—and singular—vision, the independent cinematic 'cousins' place her film as part of a continuum rather than as an isolated example of aesthetic and social progress.

Creating an Alternative Vision

Without arguing from an essentialist perspective, it is fair to trace the roots of 1990s female filmmaking to two different tendencies evident almost two decades earlier. On one end of the spectrum, experimental filmmaking sought to break the patriarchal conventions of genre, storytelling and representation. Frequently the mode was anti-realist, invoking a Brechtian stance to address the viewer directly on the social construction of sexuality, identity and roles in society. Yvonne Rainer's *Film about a Woman Who . . .* (1974) offers a paradigm for this approach. The film presents a series of situations connected to female and male/female interactions and role-playing. Using tropes from melodrama and soap opera, Rainer seeks to destabilize expectations from social situations and to make transparent the inner feelings, emotions and stresses which women have been socialized to repress. The result is a filmic text which connects with viewers on an intellectual level about emotions and social expectations. The shift away from the traditional 'pleasures' of narrative creates a much different viewing experience for viewers. As David E. James describes it, the film operates in a self-conscious mode to connect with the viewer: 'As a feature-length citation (rather than representation) of personal obsession, *Film about a Woman Who . . .* cues the distance from illusionist narrative codes that is the art film's own space of self-consciousness, and, in fact, it fragments diegetic unity more radically than any but the most analytic of Godard's films' (1989: 330). More than forty years on, Rainer's work speaks to viewers since the creative means of self-expression require an engagement that is active, questioning and present. A viewer is forced to create meaning since the traditional, and comfortable, codes of narrative, genre and social roles are no longer present.

Soon after Rainer was creating a space for female filmmakers based on anti-illusionism, a few other female filmmakers were operating closer to the mainstream of Hollywood filmmaking. Claudia Weill, for instance, generated much media attention with her film *Girlfriends* (1978). Written by Vicki Polon, *Girlfriends* details a month in the life of two friends, Susan and Anne. Susan, a photographer barely making a living, must contend with Anne moving out of their shared apartment when she moves in with her boyfriend. The film presents a lightly comic 'slice-of-life' based around balancing work life, romantic relationships and personal friendships. *Girlfriends* is not structured around key dramatic or comedic turning points. Instead, the film follows a very loose narrative dictated by the ebb and flow of real-life situations in all their messiness, confusion and complexity. The 'drama' created by Anne's departure is presented as just one of many issues that Susan negotiates with charm and self-deprecating humor. The accumulation of small incidents and the strong focus on representing Susan's daily existence make the film a compelling character study. Weill's focus on Susan is helped immeasurably by the warmth and comic flair of lead actress Melanie Mayron. *Girlfriends* presents a story that is small, intimate and centered on a character who would be absent from most mainstream Hollywood films of the time. If represented at all in a studio film, Susan would be recast in a supporting role as a wise-cracking 'best friend' whose own life would not warrant attention as the real focus of the script. Weill followed up *Girlfriends* with the bigger budget, star driven (Jill Clayburgh, Michael Douglas) romantic comedy *It's My Turn* (1980). Like *Girlfriends*, *It's My Turn* confounds expectations by focusing on a heroine, this time a mathematics professor, engaging with ongoing personal, professional and familial situations.

Both the tendencies represented by Rainer and Weill create a space for female representation missing from studio and patriarchal filmmaking. The means to that end are, however, very different: anti-illusionist storytelling devices compared to highlighting everyday lives and the situations usually deemed unworthy of dramatizing. The former were supported in experimental and avant-garde film circles, with attention from college courses, art galleries, and museum spaces. The latter developed through the 1980s as a small thread within independent cinema, with female filmmakers such as Nancy Savoca (*True Love* (1989)), Joan Micklin Silver (*Crossing Delancey* (1988)) and Joyce Chopra (*Smooth Talk* (1985)) continuing the mission of dramatizing the quotidian. Women working in the mainstream industry were very few, with Amy Heckerling (*Fast Times at Ridgemont High* (1982)) and Susan Seidelman (*Desperately Seeking Susan* (1985)) having some box office success in the comedy genre. As Christina Lane points out, however, the ability to leverage these 'calling card' successes into a long-term, sustained filmmaking career was extremely limited (2005: 196).

By the 1990s, independent cinema reached its last 'golden period' with a steady stream of auteur-driven films designed to meet both the theatrical and home markets. While this is usually equated with Quentin Tarantino, Wes Anderson, Hal Hartley and the Coen Brothers, both strands of female filmmaking grew during this period. On the realist side, Michael Z. Newman notes that some independent films of this time shift away from narrative goals/cause and effect (2011: 89). He characterizes this as 'indie realism,' replacing character traits and complexity with narrative structures of traditional modes of classical Hollywood storytelling. Nicole Holofcener's *Walking and Talking* (1996) is representative of this indie realism. In many ways, the film follows a 'next generation' example of *Girlfriends*. *Walking and Talking* tells of two late 20s female friends Laura and Amelia living in New York, focusing on their personal and professional lives and their ability to maintain a friendship despite threats around them. As Newman notes on the film's structure, 'The setup of the film, approximately its first half hour, articulates clear character traits and relationships and situations, but those goals that are presented are rather general and their pursuit is hardly systematic' (101). Joined by other female directors such as Tamara Jenkins and Allison Anders, these indie films continued to shine a light on a female protagonist and targeted lifestyle issues that were missing in mainstream studio cinema.

The experimental side of the equation was fostered through a wide variety of influences in the early 1990s. Using a Fisher Price Pixelvision camera, teenager Sadie Benning produced ten short videos from 1989 to 1992 that addressed her experience as a lesbian adolescent living and dreaming in Milwaukee. With the technical limitations of the Pixelvision camera yielding images in an ultra-grainy, unpolished black-and-white, the videos remain bold for their ability to encapsulate both the everyday experience and the fantastic longings of a young queer girl.[1] The mode of production and the self-expression represent, as Felicity Colman suggests, 'subversion to the cinematic genre of "male geniuses"' (2005: 365). At the same time as Benning's 'home movies' were making an intervention in the video and art worlds, critic B. Ruby Rich dubbed 'the New Queer Cinema' to unify several films which addressed issues of queer identity, sexuality and social transgression in the context of innovative narrational and storytelling devices (1992: 30–34). Crafted during an era when the AIDS crisis had created even higher stakes for LGBTQ representation, the New Queer Cinema used formal experimentation to establish a space to argue against repressive perspectives and views. So, for instance, Todd Haynes's juxtaposition of three tales of social marginalization in *Poison* (1991), Tom Kalin's anachronistic retelling of the Leopold/Loeb murder trial in *Swoon* (1992), and Derek Jarman's conflating of AIDS activism with imagined history in *Edward II* (1992) broke the mode of classical Hollywood storytelling time and again with bold narrational strategies. Time, space and the illusion of a contained cinematic world were adjusted as needed to address social and sexual roles.

Reclaiming the Female Voice: Three Key Texts

By the mid-1990s, these influences—realist, anti-illusionist, queer cinema—started to create richer, more textured representations of female sexuality. Aspects of all these influences began to problematize the patriarchal representations of female sexuality still so prevalent in the teen romantic comedies and dramas of that period. While I am not arguing that Sofia Coppola borrowed stylistically or narratively from any of these examples, I do believe that the terrain for a more expansive view of adolescent sexuality was present. This terrain allowed Coppola to craft her own view of adolescent female sexuality first in her short film *Lick the Star* and then in her debut feature *The Virgin Suicides*. Coppola evidences a nuanced view of adolescent sexuality, kinship and familial pressures in *The Virgin Suicides*. Three female directors' debuts in the mid-1990s also realized visions that are close to Coppola's and that suggest new ways to consider to understand female sexuality. In turn, Kelly Reichardt's *River of Grass* (1994), Jennifer

Montgomery's *Art for Teachers of Children* (1995) and Lisa Krueger's *Manny & Lo* (1996) offer glimpses of female transgression and the power of female sexuality that are allied with the aesthetic and thematic mission of Coppola.

Kelly Reichardt's debut feature *River of Grass* illustrates, in exacting detail, the misadventure of Floridian suburban housewife Cozy. Named after her father's favorite jazz musician Cozy Cole, the heroine is a stay-at-home mom stuck in a loveless marriage and too much time on her hands. Reichardt paints Cozy in a large number of unusual and vivid details. We learn that she is simply not maternal (she offers a milk bottle with Coke to her infant daughter). As Cozy explains, she would be very happy for a couple in a station wagon to pull up and just take her children away. The first section of the film, guided by Cozy's voice-over, is shaped by the small fantasies and reveries Cozy indulges in to pass her day. We see, for example, Cozy enacting a gymnastic routine, imagining an alternate reality where she would be a prize gymnast. Escaping to a nearby bar across the freeway, Cozy establishes a gentle banter, hardly even a flirtation, with Lee, a local underachiever still living at home in his late 20s. Playing with Lee's gun in a neighbor's yard, Cozy, by mistake, shoots toward the house just as the owner opens the glass door to the patio. Cozy and Lee, expecting the worst, hole up in a fleabag motel.

While this outline suggests a couple-on-the-run caper film, Reichardt presents a much different vision of both the narrative trajectory and her heroine. *River of Grass* is distinguished, first of all, by Reichardt's careful and exact presentation of space. Anchored by moving camera shots of the Florida suburbs, Reichardt presents a world of similar, barren lower middle class suburban homes, blank and empty. Characters are contained by space and engulfed by it. Reichardt is careful to shoot the film with her leads as just a small part of the open landscape. Once this vision is set, Cozy's home and especially the motel for the 'criminal couple' are sketched with perfect strokes, filled with details to create a rich sense of the atmosphere of dread facing Cozy. Reichardt establishes that space becomes action in the film. In the motel, Cozy and Lee can barely afford the daily $20 lodging fee, and are stuck due to a complete lack of funds and commitment for how to proceed. Instead of action and forward movement, Cozy is forced to consider her 'new world' of the motel, lounging on the bed, watching TV, and scurrying from Palmetto bugs in the bathroom (see Figure 1.1). So, *River of Grass* becomes a genre movie without following through on the genre story, a road movie stalled in one place, and a love story where the couple openly detest each other.

Derailing viewer expectations is crucial to the film. This applies as much to the female protagonist as to the genre and story conventions. Cozy defies

Figure 1.1 Cozy trapped in the motel room, *River of Grass* (1994)

the traditional cinematic heroine mode: she is modest, slow in speech and action, and defined by her discontent rather than by goals and aspirations. Reichardt's most formidable achievement in the film is to offer this female protagonist whose interior life is so rich and who is so at odds with the path offered to her by society and by her family. For Reichardt, the key was to make the heroine outside the domain of mainstream cinema, starting with the physical dimension: 'It gives the audience a break—especially if you're a woman to see a woman in a lead role with a body and face you can relate to. The window of what makes a woman beautiful seems to get smaller and smaller' (Reichardt and Haynes 1995: 14). Reichardt makes Cozy realize that the roles offered by life fail to meet so many of her expectations. Cozy is resolute in her determination to change her lot in life (she murmurs about falling into her 'life in crime' even while having committed nothing more than a misdemeanor). Ultimately, Reichardt underlines that Cozy does not have the power to do so. She is constrained by social roles and even by her 'partner-in-crime' Lee who imagines a new life together long after that opportunity has passed. In the film's sardonic climax, Cozy fires the gun into space again, startling Lee who jumps from their moving car. Cozy is returned to her interior life, and probably her family as well. At least she has excised Lee and his nonsense from her existence. Unlike other films, Reichardt pivots to undermine all the generic expectations, choosing instead to foreground a female protagonist whose everyday life is restricted by social norms but who plays out strong transgressions in her fantasies and imagination.

Jennifer Montgomery's *Art for Teachers of Children* similarly confounds viewer expectations in its narrative development and character psychology. Based on Montgomery's own life and her relationship with photographer Jock Sturges, the film concerns 'Jennifer,' a 14-year-old boarding school student who begins a sexual relationship with her school counselor, amateur photographer John. John also takes nude photographs of Jennifer, and other students, during the course of the film. Fifteen years after these initial events, the FBI begins an investigation over child pornography associated with the old photographs. Jennifer is contacted to testify against John, but she refuses to cooperate.

Just as *River of Grass* creates a different space for female sexuality so does Montgomery's film. The most obvious 'read' on the situation would be to portray John as a pedophile and Jennifer as the injured adolescent, scarred for life by the experiences. Montgomery complicates this scenario considerably. She includes a scene of Jennifer talking to her roommate and making decisive plans to lose her virginity ('it's about time'). Jennifer is the one who propositions John, using him as an accomplice in the act of her own deflowering. While he hesitates for a couple of hours, John soon complies with Jennifer's wishes and an affair ensues. They also begin to document Jennifer's naked body in stark black-and-white photographs. As the fictional Jennifer recounts in her voice-over, 'John liked the pictures we took together. They were never obscene—only limited by the imagination of a 14-year-old.' Her agency, somewhat limited by her youth, in the exchange is foregrounded, as is her ability to manipulate John emotionally and psychologically. Jennifer asks him, for instance, to evaluate the bodies of her schoolmates. This is designed as a way to engage John sexually and to prove her superiority over the others. Montgomery does not simply reverse the power dynamics though. Jennifer explains the lines of authority in the relationship as 'I watched him watching me and I watched my body grow.' The adult Jennifer confides to her mother that the earlier affair caused her pain and that she had asked John to apologize. The emotional suffering does not compromise either her current personality or her ability to separate John's artistic photos from 'child porn.' In sum, Jennifer embodies a complicated relationship to her sexuality from her adolescence. Quick judgments about power, agency or control over sexuality do not conform to Jennifer's lived experience in the film.

The film's style alternates between two modes: analysis of the nude photographs set against a voice-over by Jennifer and realistic, 'faux documentary' tableaux. The former functions as direct commentary on the action and issues raised over adolescent sexuality. More specifically Montgomery bookends her film with montage sequences of the photographs matched with her voice-over. The first places the photos against Jennifer (fictional or filmmaker?) reading a legal release dismissing her claims against the adult photographer. The second uses photographs of the nude adolescent Jennifer Montgomery with a voice-over explaining that these images are no longer representative of her since 'our bodies replace themselves on a molecular level.' These sequences work to implicate the viewer in these views of underage sexuality (we are confronted directly with the pictures).

At the same time though, Montgomery suggests that she/we must view the images from a distance, either through the shield of legal release or through realizing that these body images have no linkage to her current body. Thus, the viewer is left in the unusual position of being implicated in and released from these images of beauty and of exploitation. Shot at the no-budget cost of $35,000, the film's documentary-like tableaux also create an uncomfortable position for the viewer. Each setting (e.g., John's study, Jennifer's dorm room, the phone booth where adult Jennifer calls her mother) uses the same shooting setup, with no cutaways or standard shot/reverse shot mechanisms. These limitations give the film a 'security camera' feel, making the images more realistic than would be achieved using the traditional methods of cinematic storytelling. It's difficult for a viewer to engage emotionally with these characters when the rhetorical means to establish identification with the characters and their situations are withheld. Ultimately, Montgomery's film reclaims the power and potency of her young female protagonist through suggesting that female sexuality cannot be contained or captured, in an underage relationship, a nude photograph or a crusade against an alleged pedophile.

River of Grass and *Art for Teachers of Children* begin to create a space for female sexuality outside the norms of conventional Hollywood narrative. These experiments are continued in Lisa Krueger's comedy *Manny & Lo*. Unlike *Art for Teachers of Children*, *Manny & Lo* creates a linear storyline. Sisters raised in separate foster homes, 16-year-old Lo (Aleksa Palladino) and 11-year-old Manny (Scarlett Johansson) go on the run, becoming petty robbers and taking to sleeping in empty model homes. Their existence is strangely idyllic until Lo realizes that she is in her second trimester of an unplanned pregnancy. In a curious turn of events, Lo and Manny kidnap a maternity store clerk Elaine (Mary Kay Place) to help with the preparations for the new baby. The film then focuses on the unusual new family in place. Rather than escaping or fighting her new charge, Elaine eventually becomes happily complicit in the lives of Manny and Lo. Eventually this leads to Elaine 'protecting' the new family unit to outside threats and, of course, acting as a doula for the new addition to the family.

The film is pitched as a dark comedy, with large amounts of whimsy and sometimes fantastic leaps in logic. Nevertheless, *Manny & Lo* actually presents an alternative to the nuclear family through its vision of a female-centered family unit. While the unit is forged initially through the hostile action of kidnapping, soon after all three fall into their 'family roles': Elaine offering practical advice on living for both girls; Lo organizing their hideaway and protecting their space from outsiders; Manny acting as the kind and gentle mediator between Elaine and Lo. The ending suggests that the trio's alliance will continue beyond the birth of Lo's baby. If the heroine of *River of Grass* wanted a new life but could not make it a reality, *Manny & Lo* illustrates one way out. Rather than diminish or compromise the new family unit of the film, director Lisa Krueger endorses it by suggesting that, together, the trio just might be the family that each of them desired but never thought possible. In that way, the comedy presents an alternative world in which women live beyond patriarchy. Quietly, but forcefully, Krueger offers a feminist portrait, particularly of the power of young female sexuality, unlike any other up to that time.

Taken together, these three films suggest a path created by female filmmakers in the mid-1990s. Unlike the earlier non-narrative work of Rainer or the realist aesthetic of Weill, these female filmmakers present the transgressive power of female sexuality. Instead of placing these representations outside narrative filmmaking, these filmmakers developed ways to incorporate different visions of young female sexuality within independent narrative moviemaking. Expectations on gender role and narrative trajectory were cast aside by these filmmakers. Reflecting strategies in the New Queer Cinema of that decade, these films embraced bold narrational choices that spoke of the power of female sexuality. Reichardt, Montgomery and Krueger demonstrated that a female vision could operate outside the expectations and orientations of conventional Hollywood storytelling. In their films, female sexuality would be foregrounded for oppositional power. The female figure could arrest the narrative, change the course of the story, or create new social formations. The commercial space of independent cinema of the 1990s allowed these visions to be realized. Certainly female filmmakers were a small, but consistent, pulse during the boom of 1990s independent cinema. Sofia Coppola was poised to build on these efforts with her short and feature length debuts.

Lick the Star: The Virgin Suicides Diorama

Shot in 1998, Coppola's 14 minute black-and-white short, *Lick the Star*, serves as a perfect 'test pattern' for many of the stylistic flourishes and themes in *The Virgin Suicides*. Written with Stephanie Hayman, the short begins in the familiar location of a sun-drenched Southern California high school. The film examines the ebb and flow of power within a tight knit group of junior high schoolgirls (see Figure 1.2). Chloe, the queen bee,

Figure 1.2 The clique in Sofia Coppola's *Lick the Star* (1998)

hatches a plan to 'weaken' the boys by lacing their food with arsenic. The idea is borrowed from the novel *Flowers in the Attic* which the girls are studying in English class. An off-hand comment ('Nadine might have been a slave . . .') from Chloe shifts to something more sinister ('Nadine should be a slave . . .'). Chloe is branded as a racist, and simultaneously her poisoning plan is revealed. Power shifts again in the clique. As the voice-over narration concludes, 'Everything changes. Nothing changes. The tables turn and life goes on.' The hierarchy is adjusted, but it remains as potent as ever in defining status, class and position in this junior high world.

The short anticipates many of Coppola's visual stylistics and thematic pre-occupations. Coppola alternates between perfectly composed, aesthetically pleasing static shots of the girls individually or in groups with shots of movement through space. The black and white images shot by Lance Acord suggest glossy fashion photography rather than low budget guerilla filmmaking. Coppola is fond of overhead shots of the teen group lying on the lawn. The perspective flattens the image and separates the individuals rather than joining them together through match cuts. The other defining stylistic trait can be seen in Coppola's introduction of Chloe: moving in slow motion through the hallmark, the medium shots of Chloe are interrupted by extreme close-ups of her lips, her eyes and other parts of her face. These shots of characters moving through space are juxtaposed with new wave music by The Go-Gos, The Amps and Free Kitten. The effect of sound and image is to evoke the early days of music video from the 1980s despite the short being set in the late 1990s.

Thematically, *Lick the Star* operates around the shifting power struggles in the junior high student world. Coppola structures the film around the relationship between the individual (Chloe, Kate) and the group. While the individual may be striving to break free from the group, the group mindset is always present to offer a place for each of the individuals. The film isn't a 'mean girls' story, but rather a more nuanced view of how power is maintained and dispersed within a female group. In fact, the short confounds expectations as the designation of girls as 'good' or 'evil' is remarkably fluid, a single girl may occupy either role depending on the circumstances and the moment in junior high school. Even in defeat, the girls still recognize the power and role of the female group as a means of self-definition. Coppola creates a narrative in which female sexuality is at the center, but uncontained by the male gaze or male desire. For Coppola, this world is immersed in popular culture and, to some extent, defined by it. Apart from the litany of 1980s new wave anthems, the short is filled with references to consumerism, mass culture, and tabloid television. Even the phrase 'lick the star' is appropriated by the girls from the pulp horror novel *Flowers in the Attic*. Life in the high school world of *Lick the Star* is mediated, first and foremost, by brands, consumerism and pop culture.

The Virgin Suicides in the Context of 1990s Female Indie Cinema

Near the end of *Lick the Star*, Chloe's attempted suicide is shown with a haunting image of her sinking slowly into the bathtub after overdosing. The image provides the most direct link to *The Virgin Suicides*: the film opens with the youngest sister Cecilia's bathtub suicide attempt, slit wrists and a playing card of the Virgin Mary. The image breaks the tranquility of the suburban neighborhood Coppola has just so carefully pictured through shots of the homes, backyards and daily activities. The shot sets in motion the stylistics of *The Virgin Suicides*, and draws upon *Lick the Star* and the contributions of the earlier 1990s female auteurs (Reichardt, Montgomery, Krueger).

Certainly, Jeffrey Eugenides' novel is absolutely key to Coppola's adaptation of *The Virgin Suicides*. Coppola sticks closely to the book's action, even using direct phrases and narration from the book as part of her film. The directorial choices and especially the elements of cinematic style are all Coppola's, however. Further, the salient cinematic techniques draw upon the female independent history of the past invoking realist, anti-illusionist and even queer cinema techniques. At first glance, the tale of the Lisbon family and the eventual demise of all five Lisbon daughters may appear to be a family melodrama wrapped in the trauma of adolescent sexuality, religious overtones and mental illness. Placing *The Virgin Suicides* in this trajectory is less effective in understanding the film than making the links to the 1990s independents and the specific interventions of female directors in that era.

Drawing from these influences, *The Virgin Suicides* relies heavily on self-conscious cinematic flourishes set against a vivid background of the quotidian life of a single family. Like Reichardt and Montgomery, Coppola presents female sexuality in a manner that cannot be reconciled by patriarchy. *The Virgin Suicides* is a film that is based on retaining the power and the mystery of young female sexuality. The film can be seen as a failed attempt by the boys turned middle-aged men to understand the Lisbon sisters. Given their age, the boys' obsession is translated into a more general one of trying to understand the female sex. Coppola suggests through several devices in the film that the girls—and their sexuality—are forever a mystery to the boys. Therein, lies their power and ability to fascinate.

Like Reichardt, Montgomery and Krueger, Coppola unfolds her narrative in patterns that do not lend themselves to easy cooptation by genre or convention. In particular, the generic patterns and structures thrown away in Reichardt's film ('the road movie that never goes on the road') also fail to constrain Coppola. Whether tagged as a teen romance, family melodrama or mental illness drama, *The Virgin Suicides* refuses to pay off on the traditional narrative patterns and trajectories. Certainly, elements of each are invoked, but the narrative does not follow the expected track. For Coppola, *The Virgin Suicides* is instead a story that is based in female sexuality and the ways that society attempts to rationalize and control its power. Following the 1990s female indie directors, Coppola retains the beauty and mystery of female sexuality, suggesting that it can never be fully understood or recuperated by patriarchy.

Following very much in the 'test case' of *Lick the Star*, the style of *The Virgin Suicides* is dominated by strong visual flourishes. Often these stylistics are self-conscious in nature. The elements of observational cinema, rich in detail of the female adolescent life and sexuality, mirror Montgomery's bold style. Part of her project is to portray life and sexuality in an unfiltered manner. Coppola's stylistic strategies also work, however, to align the viewer with the experience of the Lisbon sisters and cement the time/place clearly in the mid-1970s upper Mid-West. Echoing both the style of New Queer Cinema and music videos, Coppola etches a vision of suburbia that is broken by reveries, dreams and flights of fancy. Coppola is aided substantially by a shifting perspective in the film; sometimes we do not know whether a scene is 'real,' a fiction, a dream or some kind of alternate reality imagined by the middle-aged narrator. Trip Fontaine's entrance, for instance, is clearly a type of fantasy rendering: he walks through the hallway of the school, girls swoon in slow motion, and the soundtrack offers 'Magic Man' by Heart. These fantasies are anchored by bold filtered visions of life matched with either banal pop music of the era or voice-over narration. These imaginative 'breaks' from reality are, in fact, deliberate to alternately align the viewer with the girls or with the boys' perceptions of the girls' reality.

Thematically and stylistically, Coppola's work in *The Virgin Suicides* follows in the trajectory of 1990s independent cinema. The self-conscious techniques, uncompromised presentation of female sexuality and thwarted expectations for narrative development follow from the female filmmakers working earlier in the decade. Reichardt, Mongomery and Krueger, among others, forged a path for the ways through which Coppola conceived and presented her female heroines. Eugenides gave Coppola her framework, but the indie female filmmakers opened the space for Coppola to present the Lisbon sisters in such an unusual and uncompromised manner. Other influences—social, commercial, aesthetic—are clearly at play in Coppola's adaptation, however. At the very end of a decade when female filmmakers started to make inroads and question the conventionality of narrative, genre, and, of course, the power of female sexuality, *The Virgin Suicides* not only continues but deepens these artistic experiments.

Note

1. For a useful discussion of Sadie Benning's aesthetic, see Benning and Smith (1998: 28–33).

2 Next Gen Coppola
Legacy, Loss and the Burden of Biography

As the daughter of one of America's leading 20th century filmmakers, Francis Ford Coppola, Sofia Coppola's early life was filtered, for better or worse, through that lens. This image shifted considerably with the debut of *The Virgin Suicides* and even more with Sofia's Best Screenplay Academy Award for *Lost in Translation*. To understand Sofia Coppola's artistry and vision for *The Virgin Suicides*, it is necessary, however, to invoke her heritage, her family ties, and especially her introduction to the world of public culture. This level of biographical detail correlates in several ways with Coppola's filmmaking style. Keeping in mind that biographic criticism is frequently singled out as a reductive method, I want nevertheless to show how Coppola's past opens up a range of emotional and social concerns that inflect the films.[1] So much of the cultural criticism of Coppola has derived from her use of costume and mise-en-scène. Indeed, she is a master at using these elements in a significant dramatic way. I want to suggest, however, that comprehending the value of Sofia Coppola to *The Virgin Suicides*, and her later films, is enriched by understanding key aspects of her biography and, in particular, the ways through which the public learned of Coppola prior to her directorial debut. As such, this 'next gen Coppola' has been shaped by her family background, especially through defining moments of grief, mourning and shaming from her largely visible past. In this way, Sofia Coppola's history created a means for an engagement with the Jeffrey Eugenides novel, and a path to illuminate the narrative with emotional complexity and depth.

Growing Up Coppola on Screen: Family & Representation

The Virgin Suicides is a story of memory: looking back twenty-five years ago, the middle-aged men attempt, unsuccessfully, to piece together the reasons for the death of the Lisbon sisters. Faded incidents, irrelevant exhibits, and vague evidence combine to make the exploration both poignant and frustrating. By the end of *The Virgin Suicides*, book and film, the audience is left with several potential explanations for the horrific events. The answers are not, however, definitive. In the same way, reviewing the biography of Sofia Coppola remains a suggestive exploratory enterprise. Her past unlocks certain concepts and emotional textures present in *The Virgin Suicides*, but it does not fully explain Sofia Coppola's creative impulse. Biographical criticism at its core is invested in the elements of an author's life as the main tenets for the critic. As Steven Lynn suggests, querying the biography of an author 'encourages you to be creative in speculating about the motivations of characters, authors or readers' (2008: 8). The process uncovers different ways to consider entry points into the film, and particularly the reasons why Coppola connected so strongly to the original source material.

Francis Coppola once proclaimed that 'film is our family business' (Aftab 2010). Many of the Coppolas—father, mother, children and relations—connects either directly or indirectly to filmmaking. Wife Eleanor documented several of her husband's films through film and memoirs (e.g., *Notes* (1979) and she directed the feature *Paris Can Wait* (2016). Sister Talia was cast as Corleone daughter Connie in *The Godfather* saga, and continued a high profile acting career for over three decades. Nephew Nicolas (Cage, then Coppola) appeared in several of his uncle's films including *Rumble Fish* (1983), *The Cotton Club* (1984) and *Peggy Sue Got Married* (1986). Born in 1971, Sofia played against gender as Michael's son being baptized in *The Godfather* (1972). Throughout her childhood and adolescence, Sofia continued to be cast by her father in roles, sometime just bit parts (a begging child gunned down in *The Cotton Club*) and other times more substantial (*Rumble Fish*, *Peggy Sue Got Married*). Francis simply enjoyed seeing Sofia on screen; as he commented about the process, 'It's like a grandiose way to have home movies.'[2]

Sofia Coppola's part in *Rumble Fish* offers a good approximation of how Francis Coppola viewed his daughter in larger roles. Sofia, aged 11 at the time of filming (and credited as 'Domino'), plays Donna, the sister of Patty (Diane Lane), girlfriend to the dim-witted gang leader Rusty James (Matt Dillon). Donna acts wise beyond her years, making jokes and gags that are more sophisticated than any of the exchanges between the older characters. She is also ultra-aggressive in sexualizing her older sister's boyfriend: Donna steals a kiss on his cheek (see Figure 2.1), snuggles up to Rusty James on the sofa, and flirts with him throughout the film. Given her age (she is obviously about five years younger than either Rusty James or Patty), the effect is more precocious than anything else. Still, the net impact is somewhat perplexing: it feels as if Francis was so charmed by the intelligence and savvy of his young daughter that he allowed her to play

Figure 2.1 Sofia Coppola (aka Domino) steals a kiss in *Rumble Fish* (1983)

with free reign in his film. Somehow the charm feels constructed however, with father giving daughter close-ups and screen time far beyond her narrative function in the film. This scenario is repeated three years later, with Sofia playing Peggy Sue's younger sister Nancy in *Peggy Sue Got Married*. While the overt sexuality is diminished, the character is reminiscent of the one from *Rumble Fish*: smart, wise, verbal and somewhat annoying and irritating in her aggressive demeanor. Both characters are typed as competitive with their older sister, with the younger sibling largely winning through smarts and a friendly antagonism.

Father and daughter collaborated on the 'Life Without Zoe' segment of the omnibus film *New York Stories* (1989): Francis and Sofia cowriting the screenplay, Sofia designing the costumes and Francis directing. In a kind of homage to the Eloise books, the Coppolas imagine an uber-wealthy 12-year-old girl (Heather McComb) living by herself in the Sherry-Netherland Hotel, just off Central Park in New York City. Her parents are almost always traveling far from New York: the father, played by Giancarlo Giannini, is an acclaimed flutist, and the mother, played by (aunt) Talia Shire is a world-class adventure photographer. The film is held together by a slender plot involving a stolen diamond, befriending an even richer middle-eastern student, and dealing with the eventual reconciliation of Zoe's estranged parents. The impulse behind the film was linked to the Coppolas' own lives (Lindsay 2004: 140). Sofia Coppola describes the parallels clearly in recounting her own life at Zoe's age, 'We lived in the Sherry-Netherland at the time and I went to school at Fieldston (the school Zoe

attends in the film)' (Sajbel 1989). Francis admits that the heroine is patterned loosely on Sofia at that age (Phillips and Hill 2004: 140). As Jon
Lewis describes Coppola's filmmaking at this time, 'Life Without Zoe' is
'both transparently and purposefully autobiographical' (1995: 147).

The film privileges conspicuous consumption above all else. 'Life Without Zoe' is centered on Zoe's daily routines: being catered to by her personal
butler Hector, taking a cab to school, hosting mocktail parties for her friends,
and so on. The film's adoration of high-end couture brands is laced throughout the characters and the action. Zoe's school t-shirt is adorned with an
oversized Chanel logo as if to emphasize the importance of the brand for Zoe
and her friends. The climax of the film takes place at a children's costume
ball. Sofia Coppola's costume designs in the ball evidence incredible detail
and most creative execution, with children in perfect replicas of everyone
from Andy Warhol and Edie Sedgwick to Elvis Presley and Cleopatra. Like
the Sofia-designed credit cartoons listing only the first name of each con-
tributor, the clothing and mise-en-scène are self-conscious in the extreme.

The film's devotion to society's top 1% occurs at the same time as an
inversion of social roles: the children are treated as adults, while the adults
(especially Zoe's mother and father) are there to receive orders, direction
and guidance from their children. So, for instance, when Zoe hears that her
parents are attempting to reconcile, she pretends to faint and counsels them
to stay broken up. The overall effect is to empower the pre-teen who is so
out of touch that she does not even realize the array of privileges offered
to her. Again, the Sofia Coppola 'stand-in' of Zoe is painted as precocious
and 'charming,' although the charm feels way more evident for the director/
father Francis than the audience member watching the film.

Reviews were dismal for the Coppola film, especially in comparison with
the adjoining short films by Martin Scorsese and Woody Allen. Jonathan
Rosenbaum (1989), writing in *The Chicago Reader*, sums up some of the
ways that 'Life Without Zoe' was received as an indulgent failure: 'Coppola
scripted this sketch with his 17-year-old daughter Sofia, who also designed
the bizarre costumes (which, in the case of Zoe on a typical day at school,
combine ragged jeans with a Chanel hat and jacket), and part of the overall incoherence of this segment undoubtedly comes from combining the
romanticized views of New York conjured up by two generations 30 years
apart.' The net effect of the project, and Sofia's earlier appearances, is to
position Sofia as a precocious talent, indulged and promoted at every turn
by her father.

Soon after 'Life Without Zoe,' Francis Coppola agreed to direct *The
Godfather Part III* (1990), extending the storyline from his most famous
films. Winona Ryder was cast in the role of Mary, Michael Corleone's
daughter, now a young adult in the film's 1979 setting. After the production

waited for Ryder to complete shooting *Mermaids* (Richard Benjamin, 1990), she was diagnosed with exhaustion when she arrived on the Coppola set. The role was a supporting one in the film. Nevertheless, dramatically, Mary Corleone played a key role in underlining the film's narrative of family, tradition and legacy. In addition, Mary's death (the accidental victim of an assassin targeting her father) serves as the film's climax. Michael's family has been destroyed despite all his efforts to change the direction of his family's future. The role of Mary therefore is central to the functioning of the film. Rather than cast an established actress in the role, Francis Coppola decided to have his daughter Sofia play the role.

As an amateur playing against such established actors as Al Pacino, Diane Keaton, Joe Mantegna, and Eli Wallach, Sofia was placed in a vulnerable position by her father. Ex-post, Francis Coppola defended his decision by describing her casting in line with the tradition of Italian Neo-realism: 'It is true that I was using her more like an Italian Realist director would, as a real person who happens to be in a fictional situation' (quoted in Bahiana 2017). Mother Eleanor Coppola, in her autobiography, recounts the tumultuous shooting with Sofia alternately courageous, excited, tired and miserable (2008: 119). As many others noted, Eleanor Coppola questioned the judgment of her husband to place Sofia in such a high profile role given her lack of experience. The mother confided during production, 'Well-meaning people tell me I am permitting a form of child abuse' (118). She notes, however, that Francis was motivated in part by seeking parallels between the father and daughter pair, fictional and real-life. Francis supposedly could make a more resonant emotional picture through casting his own daughter in the fictional daughter role.

On release in December 1990, the film's reviews were dominated by a single recurring thread: the disastrous performance of Sofia Coppola. *Entertainment Weekly*'s cover story ('Storm over Sofia Coppola') referred to the press coverage as 'one of the nastiest Hollywood controversies in years' (Gerosa 1991: 13). Critics took aim at Sofia's 'Valley Girl' accent, her bland line readings, and her utter lack of emotional range. The dramatic climax of Mary's death elicited laughter rather than pathos from some critics at screenings. Most critics were laser focused on demolishing the young actor's acting prospects. A few, surprisingly Pauline Kael among them, defended the choice; as Kael explains, 'It's obvious that this teen-age girl is not a trained actress; she seems uncomfortable at times, and her voice (or a dubber's voice) lacks expressiveness—which is a serious flaw in her last scene. But she has a lovely and unusual presence; she gives the film a breath of life, and I grew to like her' (2017).

Certainly, these reviews should be seen in the context of Francis Coppola's career. In many ways, Sofia Coppola's negative reviews are simply collateral damage from the press turning on Francis. Claims of nepotism are obvious, and are even more pressing given the quality of her performance. It is worth considering other factors at play in the critical reception though. The sum of Sofia's other performances and her creative role in the poorly received 'Life Without Zoe,' no doubt, contributed to the critics' response to her role as Mary. Some of the reaction may be due to the hubris on the part of both father ('*she* can play this role') and daughter ('I *can* play this role'). Other responses seem located more squarely on the shoulders of Francis. The film was released 16 years after the first sequel, and after a period of much financial and critical turmoil: the huge personal commercial failure of *One from the Heart* (Francis Ford Coppola, 1982), the sale of Coppola's Zoetrope Studios and a decade with a track record with far more 'misses' (*Rumble Fish* (1983), *The Cotton Club* (1984), *Gardens of Stone* (1987), *Tucker: The Man and His Dreams* (1988), 'Life Without Zoe') than hits (*The Outsiders* (1983), *Peggy Sue Got Married* (1986)). Francis' choice to reboot the Godfather series was seen by many as a way to cash in on his highest moment of commercial and critical triumph. As such, the decision to make the third film could be interpreted as both commercially pragmatic and as meddling with two true American masterpieces of cinema. Critics who were looking for reasons to critique *The Godfather Part III* were handed by Francis Coppola its greatest vulnerability, the performance by his daughter. In this way, the vitriol of the critics, while focused on Sofia, was actually directed at her father for tampering with a near-perfect pair of films with the unneeded sequel.

While the professional achievements of the Coppola family ebbed and flowed during the decade, the period was dark for the Coppola family on a personal basis. The close-knit family was shattered by the death of son, Gio, in May 1986. A boating accident in Maryland took the life of the 23-year-old who was working on preproduction of his father's *Gardens of Stone* (Anon 1986). Eleanor Coppola recounts the huge impact on all the family members, including 15-year-old Sofia: 'The next days are memory fragments. I can see Sofia and Roman crying on the rented sofa in the apartment . . . Francis doubled over on the floor . . . the pain of seeing the family devastated layered on my own grief' (2008: 16–17). Rather than cancel the imminent production of *Gardens of Stone*, Francis plowed ahead with the film, seeking solace in the work. Francis returned to his film despite the tragedy. The absolute importance of family above all else resonates as a theme in interviews with the director after this point. Echoing Sofia's comment, Francis sought to create a space in the 'family business' for all of his family members. In addition to Sofia's transition to director and screenwriter, brother Roman and mother Eleanor also eventually directed their own films (Shaffer 2017). Francis' production company, American Zoetrope, was given to Roman and Sofia who now operate it. American Zoetrope has been the production company behind most of the family films, regardless of distributor or financing.

Formative Experiences: Mourning and Humiliation

These events would seem to be, on the surface, scarring and potential harmful to the development of the teen and young adult Sofia. However, psychoanalytic and psychological literature suggest a different trajectory, that mourning and creativity are closely linked (Pollock 1989). Psychoanalyst Melanie Klein posits that 'reparative drives' restoring loved objects form the basis for creativity and sublimation. For Klein, mourning becomes productive at its most acute state (Klein 1940: 143). The creative process is not seen as the end point of the mourning, but rather as a working through, an attempt at 'mourning work' (ibid.). As such, mourning work can be seen as one way to move forward through loss rather than focusing on the absence of the loved one. From a psychological perspective, 'survivor guilt' over the loss of a family member inspires energy that can be channeled productively into artistic endeavors. Eleanor Coppola, for instance, developed a gallery project using cairns, a series of rock piles with each rock inspired by a regret, loss or departed friend or family member. The entire installation was a structure covered with heartfelt notes, offering a visual way to connect and commemorate in a shared fashion with others. Coppola has stated that the project was inspired by the loss of her son, whose name became the very first remembrance in the exhibition (2008: 190).

Experiencing the loss of a sibling during adolescence is understandably transformative. The adolescent's family is one of the key factors on how this transformation is realized. A family with close personal ties who communicate openly with each other often struggle through 'enduring sadness' but one that does not incapacitate their lives (Balk et al. 2017: 54). Similarly, an emotional maturity can be achieved in these circumstances, with 'vulnerability, empathy and interpersonal maturity' emerging in the aftermath of the tragedy (51). From accounts by both Eleanor and Francis, the family did become even closer after the death of Gio. *The Virgin Suicides* as a project would allow Sofia the narrative entry point to reflect on the issues of loss and grief, albeit in a much different context.

For Sofia, personal mourning was soon followed by the intense public humiliation at the hands of the press. There are several layers to this particular sense of humiliation. In some ways, the entertainment press has relied upon the structure of building up—and then breaking down—icons. This process reflects the tension Richard Dyer locates in the stardom between the 'ordinary' ('they're just like us') and the 'extraordinary' ('talent separates them from us') (Dyer 1979: 49–50). Sofia's experience with the hostile reviews can therefore be seen as part of a largely inevitable process in show business. In this case, the 'take down' was magnified by the dual target of both Sofia and her father.

As with mourning, humiliation may start in a negative space, but it does not need to finish there. Cultural critic Wayne Koestenbaum complicates our understanding of humiliation through suggesting that, in fact, the process may harbor hidden positives. As Koestenbaum suggests, 'Humiliation, an educating experience, breeds identity' (2011: 16). The process of engaging with the humiliation, and surviving it, presents the person with an opportunity to gain resilience and fortitude in presenting themselves, their ideas and their creative work. Koestenbaum focuses on the potential for growth in the face of humiliation. Secondarily, those surrounding the one humiliated have the chance to reaffirm their commitment to the person in light of the humiliation; as the author states, 'Seeing your abasement, I overflow with love' (41). Humiliation opens a space that can be used for a person to develop or simply to atrophy. Koestenbaum's main contribution is to make us rethink humiliation for offering a positive charge. Under certain circumstances, humiliation can be the means to grow more radically and forcefully than would be possible without the external 'damage.'

During her youth, Sofia Coppola's primary creative outlet had always been visual. As Francis described it, 'I saw her talent right when she was four years old designing clothes for her paper dolls.'[3] Mother Eleanor aligns her own visual filmmaking style as closer to Sofia than to her husband's: 'I think stylistically, I think I'm closer to my daughter [Sofia]. I have a strong visual sense. Francis does too, but from a more masculine perspective. I have a more feminine visual aesthetic' (Shaffer 2017). Reservations about the precocious image seemingly cultivated for Sofia by her father through her film appearances do not diminish the strength of her visual imagination. Even those who took issue with the plot of 'Life Without Zoe' admitted that the costume design and visual imagery were strong and creative. This theme would continue as Sofia became a director: critics praised the visual imagery of the films, sometimes to the detriment of the film's narrative or characters. This reading, however, is short-sighted. Understanding Coppola's biography illuminates the strains of mourning and humiliation present in the young artist. These emotional 'milestones' helped Sofia Coppola to infuse her visual sense with a depth of emotion and compassion.

The Virgin Suicides, made a full ten years after Sofia's appearance in *The Godfather Part III*, offered the ideal subject for the intersection of the emotional maturation with the visual sense. Through the source material of the Jeffrey Eugenides' book, Coppola was able to find her voice as a creative artist. The connections between Eugenides' novel and elements of Coppola's life are many. The 'mourning work' over her brother Gio is played out across two different plains. The first is through the older sisters mourning the early suicide of Cecilia. The second way is more complex: through the neighborhood boys (turned middle-aged men) narrating the 'mystery' of the Lisbon girls' suicide and mourning the girls and, even more, the death of their neighborhood, hometown and youth. The neighborhood boys' engagement with the mystery—reading Cecilia's diary, interacting with the girls through music, spying on the Lisbon home through a telescope—also represents a creative way to filter the horror of the deaths. The book seeks answers even though their process of discovery yields little in the way of explanations or motivations for the tragic event. Like the boys in *The Virgin Suicides*, Sofia is a victim of 'survivor guilt,' the syndrome attached to the survivor of the deceased sibling. Just as the boys enact their investigation, Sofia engages with survivor guilt through creating a film based on the novel that takes the psychological adjustment as one of its key subject matters. *The Virgin Suicides* allows Sofia to realize the range of emotions attached to the reflection of an untimely death. The book does not simply target grief and sorrow, but rather places these emotions in an array of other responses and reactions (e.g., satire, humor, anger, desire and repulsion).

The Virgin Suicides also connects for Coppola through the role of the family as a support and a threat. For Eugenides, the family unit is both a place for care (hosting a party for Cecilia, attempting to morph the harsh rules of the past) and torment (sequestering the girls after Lux's transgression, burning the offensive record albums). The family structure is close: in fact, the girls rarely undermine or contradict their parents, even under trying circumstances. The Lisbon sisters endure small and large humiliations at the hands of their strict parents: being forced to wear the loose-fitting robes to prom, having an early curfew, and, of course, being under the watchful eye of their father who is also the math teacher at their high school. A cursory read of the situation might propose that the girls are vexed by a domineering mother and a weak father. Eugenides tempers this through giving the mother scenes of compassion and tenderness, and the father moments of strength and clear action. A simple psychological explanation is inadequate to explain the complex dynamics within the family and its role in the lives of the Lisbon sisters. Similarly, Sofia Coppola's family must be seen as both a place for support (Francis fostering Sofia's career since childhood) and potential pain (humiliation through *The Godfather Part III*, making Sofia's childhood visible to the public through the films). Like the Lisbon family, the Coppolas are united to the outside. Even in light of her public 'shaming,' Sofia defended her father and claimed that she only cared that he was happy with her performance.

The Coppola family facilitated Sofia's first feature through Francis' production company, American Zoetrope. Eventually transferred to Sofia and her brother Roman Coppola, American Zoetrope began life for father

Francis Coppola as Zoetrope Studios in 1969. As part of the 'next genera-tion' of Coppolas, Sofia was able to utilize the structure, organization and creative talent of American Zoetrope for her debut feature. This yielded actors (e.g., Kathleen Turner, Danny De Vito, Scott Glenn, Kirsten Dunst) familiar to American Zoetrope films and creative/executive talent (producers Francis Coppola and Fred Roos, executive producer Fred Fuchs, co-editor Melissa Kent, sound designer Richard Beggs) as well. Crucially, Coppola augmented these industry veterans with creative talents early in their career, such as co-editor James Lyons, costume designer Nancy Steiner and most auspiciously the French electronic duo Air as the soundtrack composers. The American Zoetrope connection offered Sofia Coppola a 'safe harbor' to experiment aesthetically in an environment of familiar and trusted art-ists. American Zoetrope had a lengthy history of sponsoring both cinematic auteurs (Wim Wenders, Jean-Luc Godard, Hans-Jurgen Syberberg, Akira Kurosawa) and first-time directors (Caleb Deschanel, Carroll Ballard, God-frey Reggio, Victor Salva). Through American Zoetrope, *The Virgin Sui-cides* was financed independently, premiered at the Cannes Film Festival in 1999, and was picked up for domestic distribution by Paramount Classics.

The Virgin Suicides allowed Sofia to bid farewell to the image of the precocious child which had been cultivated by Francis and popular criti-cism. Immediately, the choices made by Sofia demonstrated a unique per-spective. Consider casting for the film. Certainly, Coppola was able to leverage actors who had appeared in American Zoetrope films, but the spe-cific casting choices could be 'against the grain.' Most obviously Danny DeVito, who appeared two years previously in Francis Coppola's *The Rain-maker* (1997), was cast as the psychiatrist Dr. Hornicker. Devito's diminu-tive stature, snarling personality, and quick comic wit set a strong image in such comedies as *Ruthless People* (David Zucker, Jim Abrahams and Jerry Zucker, 1986), *Throw Momma from the Train* (Danny DeVito, 1987) and *Twins* (Ivan Reitman, 1988). Even in supporting roles in largely dra-matic films, DeVito conveyed a whiff of outrage and humor. Consequently, DeVito as the psychiatrist questioning a young teen after a suicide attempt in *The Virgin Suicides* seems quizzical at first. The choice telegraphs Cop-pola's iconoclasm, pairing one of the key authority figures of her film with comic DeVito. The casting throws into question Coppola's take on the role of psychiatry and therapy in a film that will supposedly be about both.

Loss in the Style of *The Virgin Suicides*

Through the 'mourning work' of the film, Sofia's potent visual imagination was fused with a psychological and emotional investigation of loss. Rather than locate her talents on the visual level, Sofia was able to transform her gifts to become an innovative filmmaker. The extent to which Sofia was able to realize this new phase can be seen in the visual style of the film. Some have seen her strengths in visual style as compensation for a lack of interest in narrative or character (Kennedy 2010: 38–40). I would argue that this criticism is an inadequate view of Coppola's approach. She is adroit at using the visual and stylistics to evoke deep emotion and to illuminate the characters and their relationships.

Sofia Coppola has been widely praised for the visual style of her films. Fiona Handyside, for instance, sees this style as 'associated with the contemporary visual construction of girlhood' (2017: 42). Belinda Smaill, on the other hand, locates Coppola's auteurism in structures of duration, waiting and repetition within the films (2013: 148–162). *The Virgin Suicides* evidences several means to convey loss through the visual stylistics of the film. Certainly, the mise-en-scène is rich and detailed; Coppola is able to evoke the mid-1970s Michigan with specificity and care. The director harnesses the mise-en-scène to retain the central enigma of the book (i.e., why did the Lisbon sisters commit suicide?). This is accomplished through three key strategies.

First, Coppola refuses to align the viewer with key characters and the drama of their situation. As the book is told by a plural omniscient narrator (the middle-aged men recalling their youth), the tale shifts between different modes of storytelling and the reader is left unanchored, at times, over which perspective or point-of-view is being represented. Coppola retains this structure in her film. While there is only one male voice-over narrator (voiced by Giovanni Ribisi), the narrator continually refers to the plural 'we' throughout the film. In addition, the viewer does not know which boy (now middle-aged man) is narrating the film. Editor James Lyons has stated that Coppola was pressured into identifying which character was narrating, but she deliberately chose not to single out one of the boys.[4] Through reflecting the narrational structure of Eugenides' book, Coppola set in motion the more general stylistic tendency to keep the viewer at bay.

Instead of shooting the film with typical medium and close-up shots connected to the characters and their dramatic situation, Coppola uses strategies that block these methods to elicit emotion and a bond with the film. Certainly the film elicits an emotional response, but, through many choices, Coppola chooses not to deliver the expected or usual emotion from a scene or circumstance. So, for example, when Trip Fontaine (Josh Hartnett) talks to Mr. Lisbon (James Woods) about the parents' decision to take the daughters to the dance, the scene is shot through a closed door. From a small window in the door, the viewer can see Trip and Mr. Lisbon in long shot. After Mr. Lisbon proclaims, 'My wife and I have had a little talk and come to a decision on your request,' the door is closed and then the viewer cannot hear the crucial dialog concluding the scene. Coppola elides the most significant emotional 'payoff' and the way that audience would connect more closely with both Trip and Mr. Lisbon.

Similarly, Coppola uses the same strategy to shoot Cecilia's funeral. As the hearses enter the cemetery, they are met by many striking workers. Mr. Lisbon gets out to talk with the strikers. Rather than dramatize the exchange between the grieving father and the strikers, Coppola and cinematographer Edward Lachman shoot the scene through the car's windshield. The audio track is ambient music from Air, and the viewers do not hear the father's dialog with the others. The exchange is successful: the cars are allowed to enter the cemetery. The viewer, however, is left to imagine how Mr. Lisbon was able to convince the strikers to let the cars through. The emotional power of the scene is muted by design.

This strategy recurs throughout the film. Consider also the scene of Father Moody telling Mrs. Lisbon that Cecilia's death will be recorded as an 'accident' rather than as a suicide. Coppola stages this intimate scene with Father Moody entering the Lisbon bedroom. Mrs. Lisbon is seated on the bed, facing away from the camera. As Father Moody explains the news, only the back of Mrs. Lisbon, in medium shot, is visible to the camera. When he concludes, Mrs. Lisbon turns her head only and nods. The scene ends on this restrained note. Coppola's staging blocks the expected emotional connection between the characters. Instead, we are left with a curious tableaux in which emotion is drained from the scene rather than emphasized.

Second, Coppola's camera placement acts in a similar manner, to distance the viewer and to emphasize the sense of loss. Consider, for instance, two adjoining scenes. In the first, Lux wakes up on the football field. The scene begins with a medium shot on Lux, bathed in a soft blue light, with Air's ambient soundtrack playing in the background. The scene opens like a dream, with Lux waking after a night of high school triumph (becoming homecoming queen and a romance with Trip). This initial reaction is undercut considerably as the camera pulls back to reveal Lux alone on the huge football field. Trip has left hours before and she is greeted by the harsh morning light. Starting as a moment of bliss and quiet contemplation, the scene is revealed to be one of abandonment. After a brief cab ride, Lux arrives at the Lisbon home. Coppola and cinematographer Lachman cover this incident in a single long shot. The confrontation between Lux and her upset parents is barely heard. The attention in the scene is, instead, deflected to the cab backing out of the driveway (the only element in motion). The expectation would be to cover the scene with close-ups showing the intense drama between the three characters. Coppola does not allow for that conventional approach, leaving viewers searching for an emotional connection.

Not all of Coppola's strategies of loss involve limiting the viewer's access to the characters, action and drama. In fact, Coppola's adaptation makes explicit connections and parallels that are left either unstated or in the background of the Eugenides novel. The novel is incredibly detailed, with rich visual allusions and very specific references to the world of the young characters. While stunningly textured, the novel is also very much a 'memory book,' that is, it depends on the narrator/s to either offer or to recall specific incidents from the past. In an on-set interview, Eugenides explains how the actualization of the novel shifts the meaning: 'The book is not character driven at all. The only character, in a sense, is the collective narrator. You get a fragmentary knowledge of a lot of the characters— Mr. Lisbon, Mrs. Lisbon—of what they're like in the book. Now they're actually embodied by these really terrific actors. They become bigger characters than I'd imagined in the book.'[5] The details from the novel are now anchored by their physicality in the film through actors, but also through a myriad of other choices in screenplay adaptation, production design, costuming, acting style, and staging. These choices serve to emphasize Coppola's mise-en-scène of loss and regret.

This process highlights certain aspects of Eugenides' novel and leaves others unexpressed. Tellingly, Coppola is able to create a stronger 'cause and effect' based around loss compared to the book. Cecilia's party, for instance, is a key incident in both the book and film. This is the event immediately preceding Cecilia's second (and successful) suicide attempt. In the book, the narrator/s are focused on their own engagement with the party. The reader follows their navigation of the party through their interactions with the sisters and the space of the chaperoned party. This includes a detailed description of 'Joe the Retard,' to use the offensive nickname of the narrators. As they comment, 'We were happy when Joe the Retard showed up' (Eugenides 1993: 25). Their interactions with Joe are capped with 'The party was just beginning to get fun when Cecilia slipped off the stool and made her way to her mother' (26). The next incident is Cecilia throwing herself from the upstairs bedroom window.

Coppola's adaptation sticks closely to the outline of these scenes in the book. Coppola is able, however, to focus attention on the Joe interactions, showing Joe, the sisters, and the neighborhood boys huddled together. The scene plays out so that the viewer sees directly Cecilia's blank expression, refusing to foster the humiliating banter with Joe. The cramped space of the den, the vivid choices of the costuming (especially Joe's blazer and the too formal clothes of the teen boys) and the frenzied interactions between the characters all foster a greater sense of the claustrophobia and discomfort of the situation. Whereas Eugenides, speaking through the neighborhood boys, portrays the situation as light hearted and 'fun,' Coppola exposes the bullying and the sadism of the scene through her choices. With Cecilia's action directly—and quickly—after these events with Joe, Coppola suggests a stronger causation for the suicide. Eugenides offers this clue, as one among many, while Coppola's dramatization of the scene presents a different interpretation: the bullying of Joe was the 'final straw' for Cecilia, confirming her dark world view and pushing her to commit suicide. Through translating the sometimes oblique and multifaceted novel to the screen, Coppola has created a physical and temporal space for the action. This process facilitates the linear storytelling and causation in action in a way avoided by Eugenides in his novel.

These strategies—formal compositions limiting access to character and drama, cinematography doing the same, and the explicit storytelling devices used nevertheless to create a linearity in the film—all lead to the same end. The viewer becomes deeply invested in the loss of the Lisbon sisters, although this loss is engaged more on an intellectual than an emotional basis. Near the end of the film, Coppola surveys the contents of the nearly empty Lisbon home. Placed against static shots of each room and icons/artifacts (e.g., Lux's homecoming tiara, the Polaroid camera) from earlier in the film, the narrator explains, 'In the end, we had pieces of the puzzle, but no matter how we put them together, gaps remain.' Coppola's stylistic choices privilege these gaps and fissures. The loss evident through so many of the stylistic choices matches perfectly with the narrative. Even more, the style can be seen as an engagement on the biographical level. For a director whose life had been marked by mourning, humiliation and public fascination, *The Virgin Suicides* dovetails perfectly with Coppola's 'working through' the issues of her past. The stylistic choices in *The Virgin Suicides* deepen through the remainder of her career. In fact, many of the same distancing techniques recur in subsequent Coppola films (especially evident in the precise father/daughter Hollywood tale, *Somewhere* (2010)).

Notes

1. For a useful review of a variety of issues related to authorship and agency, consult Naremore (1990: 14–23).
2. Francis Coppola, director commentary accompanying the Blu-ray of *Rumble Fish* (Criterion Collection, 2017); audio commentary originally.
3. Coppola was quoted in the Commentary for the DVD of *Rumble Fish*, Special Edition, 2005, Universal Pictures Home Entertainment.
4. 'Film Editor Jim Lyons on the Amorphous Nature of "The Virgin Suicides"' *Manhattan Edit Workshop*, 23 September 2015; www.youtube.com/watch?v=g64zbmk1at0.
5. *The Virgin Suicides* 'making of' documentary, *The Virgin Suicides* DVD, 2000, Paramount.

3 The Enigma of *The Virgin Suicides*

Before diving into the narrative enigmas of *The Virgin Suicides*, it is worth considering just the title of the book and film. The title, by itself, reveals much of the approach to storytelling from both Eugenides and Coppola. Asked directly about the meaning of the title, Eugenides stresses two elements: 'The virgin has to do with religious imagery and suffering, and it's perhaps more to do with that than physical virginity. I was really thinking what those suicides might have been called in a tabloid or magazine. Obviously not all the Lisbon girls are virgins' (quoted in Myers 2013). By itself, the title is provocative without specifying the potential plot. Is the film about a violent ritual sacrificing virgins? A murder mystery? A tale of losing your virginity to your first love? Any of these readings is possible. Certainly invoking both burgeoning sexuality and death, the title announces boldly that the film will deal with two 'taboo' subjects that are designed to get a reaction from audience members. Even more, juxtaposing the two terms immediately suggests a curiosity or mystery (e.g., what is the connection with virginity and committing suicide? Why do *The Virgin Suicides* occur?). Eugenides is correct in labeling the title as 'tabloid' since it suggests a combination of (no) sex and (self) violence that is both perverse and intriguing in its mystery.

Establishing right away that the story is a mystery set largely in the past, the film opens with the title 'Michigan 25 years ago.' The narrator then links the setting to the death by suicide of the Lisbon sisters. The neighborhood boys—now middle-aged men—are still fascinated by the mass suicide. They are 'putting the pieces together' and looking at 'the evidence' of the case. As such, the film is set in motion as this process of sifting through the evidence of the girls' suicides. As Debra Shostak clarifies on the central narrative trajectory: 'The secret of the narrative lies in the girls' mysterious motivation for suicide—the why, not the what' (2009: 813). The course of the film is set. Guided by the (unspecified) male narrator, the viewer must 'solve' the mystery of the Lisbon girls' suicide. The viewer is primed to become a psychological detective, looking for clues leading to an explanation of the deaths.

Presenting the rationale and details behind the deaths fall into the realm of narration. The 'task' of any film is to offer information which is laced into storylines and drama by the viewer. As David Bordwell explains about this process, 'Narration is knowledgeable, self-conscious and communicative' (1985: 57). *The Virgin Suicides* substantially complicates this process of narration, however. While the film is constructed as a type of mystery, the development and particulars of the narration actually deviate from the general principles offered by Bordwell. Parallel films that shift the model of narration are useful to consider at this point. While these films do not follow the specific narrative pattern of *The Virgin Suicides*, all of these films are structured loosely around the 'threat' of female sexuality within a patriarchal world. In terms of her storytelling approach, Coppola does not start from ground zero. Her narration echoes not just the structure of the Eugenides book, but key cinematic examples as well.

Deceptive Mysteries: Narrational Lessons from the Past

For storytelling, several films center on negotiating a space for female sexuality in the context of a mystery. Three films, in particular, align closely with *The Virgin Suicides*: Michelangelo Antonioni's *L'Avventura* (1960), Nicolas Roeg's *Bad Timing: A Sensual Obsession* (1980), and Peter Weir's *Picnic at Hanging Rock* (1975). All three start from a place of mystery, but each offers unexpected ways to move the story forward. Most tellingly, all the strategies mobilized in these films have been integrated into Coppola's filmmaking in *The Virgin Suicides*. While the narrative content of the film hews closely to the book, the cinematic means of storytelling draw on these earlier parallels from film history.

Writing in 1961, critic Joseph Bennett summed up *L'Avventura* as concerned with 'the impossibility of communication between human beings' (432). This theme is reflected in the ways that *L'Avventura* tricks the viewer, suggesting one course of narrative action and then freely changing focus. Bold more than a half century later, *L'Avventura* plays as a modernist spin on the search for a missing friend. During an afternoon's cruise, a group of friends stops at a deserted island for some rest and relaxation. Anna, the dissatisfied girlfriend of Sandro, goes missing. Antonioni devotes screen time to the friends searching for her in the ocean and on the island. Without any discussion or explanation, the search becomes far less of a priority. The characters return to their bourgeois pursuits and their lives of luxury. Anna's best friend, Claudia, who had been with the group on the day of the disappearance soon begins a tentative affair with Sandro. This liaison is undercut by emotional and physical betrayals leading to an ending in which both Claudia and Sandro must face a bleak and compromised future. Most tellingly, by the final third of the film, the initial mystery—the key dramatic enigma—has been largely forgotten. The passivity and loose morals of the friends has led to the mystery being irrelevant to their daily lives. Structurally, the film is set up to be a mystery, but Antonioni forces his viewer to engage with the film, its characters, and their environment on an intellectual basis instead. Emotion and gratification from the standard generic and narrative conventions are of little interest to the director. The pleasures of 'solving the mystery' are taken away by Antonioni. Viewers must consider the film as a more realistic depiction of the human condition, one in which the past resists simple explanation or reconciliation.

The mystery in *Bad Timing: A Sensual Obsession* concerns an abuse of trust: a Viennese Detective Netusil (Harvey Keitel) investigates the near-death experience of a young American woman, Milena (Theresa Russell) and, in particular, the role played in the incident by her estranged psychiatrist boyfriend Alex (Art Garfunkel). As events unfold, the detective becomes convinced that Milena was ravished by Alex after she had called him to say she was committing suicide. The path of the film is to examine the timeline of events: Milena's phone call to Alex; Alex arriving at Milena's apartment; Alex finally calling for an ambulance. While Antonioni discards the mystery of his film to make a larger comment about the social environment and the ennui of his characters, Roeg takes a much different route with *Bad Timing*. As Roeg comments on his method,

> Another trigger for emotion that film can express more perfectly than any other form—especially when linked to music is memory. I loathe the term "flashback"—it has come to mean a cinematic gimmick and is generally attacked by the critics. But our memory and thoughts are constantly going backwards and forwards like a clock, tick-tock, tick-tock, tock-tick, tock-tick.
>
> (2013: 154)

Roeg filters his mystery through memory. Scenes are depicted as 'flashbacks' but the viewer soon learns that the scenes cannot be trusted. In particular, Alex may be lying to cover up the discrepancies in the timeline. The viewer sees Alex's testimony dramatized, but must weigh this against other scenes and actions that may contradict the memory. The case progresses, and Detective Netusil becomes more fascinated with Alex's psychology and his motives for the crime. So much so that, in certain flashbacks, Netusil is inserted as a voyeur to the action.[1] He looks onto the action of the past and even responds in real time. This impossible flashback, placing a new character into the memory being recounted of another character, breaks with the mode of conventional storytelling. Roeg draws attention to the flexibility and fluidity of memory, as well as to our desire to narrativize past experience. *Bad Timing* illustrates how a cinematic mystery should always be addressing perspective and reliability of the narration. Rather than simply 'believing' the events of a flashback, viewers need to understand the process of memory (the fissures, the gaps, the contradictions) and the ways through which narration can confound viewership. *Bad Timing* is a mystery in two ways, in terms of both narrative and narration. The film expands the ways we conceive of storytelling practice, moving toward narrational practice aligned with character psychology as much as realism and verisimilitude.

Picnic at Hanging Rock offers the strongest parallels to the narrational strategies of *The Virgin Suicides*. The film opens with a title card: 'On Saturday 14th February 1900 a party of schoolgirls from Appleyard College picnicked at Hanging Rock near Mt. Macedon in the state of Victoria. During the afternoon several members of the party disappeared without trace . . . .' The trailer promises 'fragments of a mystery from a summer long ago.' The word 'fragments' is absolutely key. While Weir has the story unfold in a linear time frame, there are so many potential aggressive forces at play in the disappearance that viewers can easily chart their own course on the 'why' behind the story. Explanations could involve mystical forces, sunstroke, slipping on a rock crevasse, and even foul play by one of other school friends and teachers. All of the action is placed against the setting of a secondary school for girls. An air of sexual repression and desperation is present throughout. While there is no suggestion of rape or molestation, the sexuality of the young women, all dressed in white, proves to be a powerful force motivating both the searchers and the remaining young women (see Figure 3.1).

The second half of the film recounts the (failed) search for the girls and the aftermath of those left behind. The College disintegrates under a wave of bad publicity and relationships are strained between the teachers and their students. There is no solution to the mystery of the disappearance. *Picnic at Hanging Rock* ends without specifying any answers. We are left with a film that started explicitly as a mystery, but, in its refusal to stake a claim for any one explanation, shifts to become something else: an atmospheric horror film? A study in hysteria? A folkloric tale on nascent sexuality? Weir challenges the viewers' traditional pleasures from storytelling through this unexpected road map. Like *L'Avventura* and *Bad Timing*, Weir's film uses narration that blocks, teases and misleads the viewer as much as communicates freely. These films challenge the viewer to interpret action, motivation and drama without relying on the recoupable narrative structure present in so much of cinematic fiction.

Figure 3.1 Picnic at Hanging Rock (1975): mystery and female sexuality, unreconciled

A mystery now irrelevant, perspectives multiplied, and a refusal to yield closure—all of these 'lessons' from the cinematic past reflect on Sofia Coppola's storytelling in *The Virgin Suicides*. Retaining the fissures in Eugenides' novel, Coppola translates these thwarted expectations and misleading explanations into cinematic terms. Eugenides explicitly acknowledges this structure: 'The book is a faux detective story, in a way, and so they're gathering evidence, and the exhibits are the evidence that they're gathering' (quoted in Schiff 2006: 114). Coppola does not use the same system of coded and numbered 'exhibits' in her film, but there are plenty of artifacts and narrative threads to act as clues to the mystery. Most significantly, like Eugenides, Coppola tells the story through memory, with the viewer alerted immediately to the 'suicide free-for-all.'

Who Tells the Story?

The viewer must follow the path of the neighborhood boys—now twenty-five year later, middle-aged men—who have been obsessed with the Lisbon mass suicide. Eugenides' plural 'we' of the novel becomes a single narrator in the film. The narrator begins the film with the bold proclamation, 'Everyone dates the demise of the neighborhood from the suicides of the Lisbon girls.' This statement establishes two 'truths' immediately: the importance of the Lisbon girls for the boys and the connection between the death of the girls and the overall decline of their neighborhood (city? state? lives?). The stakes are raised considerably soon after as the narrator continues, 'Now whenever we run into each other at business lunches or cocktail parties, we find ourselves in the corner going over the evidence one more time. All to understand those five girls who, after all these years, we can't get out of our minds.' The ability of the Lisbon suicides to hold the boys/men captive is therefore an admission, almost a statement of fact. It is worth thinking, however, more about the context of the boys' obsession.

Assuming that the boys were in their mid-teens when the suicides occurred, the narrator would be in his early 40s at the time of the storytelling. The gap of twenty-five years is crucial to the storytelling, as is the context of the present day discussion of the case. The comments suggest that, despite the single narrator, we will be experiencing a 'collective' mindset. If the events are being replayed, reconsidered and rethought over a twenty-five-year period, inevitably certain ones will rise to the surface, others will fall by the wayside. Memory is, of course, fallible. Only the most vivid and emotionally resonant events will become the 'established facts' of the case. So, in effect, Eugenides and Coppola telegraph through this early narration that we will be seeing a collective memory of the events. The structure places all the power in the hands of the narrator. Given the expanse of time between the original events and the narrator's tale, isn't it reasonable to expect some slippage or revision in the history? In fact, in ex-post analysis, the argument can easily be made that certain scenes have been exaggerated, others transformed, and still others shaped by the collective. All of these transformations make the storytelling more complex than it may first appear. As in *Bad Timing*, reflecting on the perspective, or who is telling the story, is crucial to understanding the structure and power of the film.

Pictured at first as four teenage boys, without differentiation, sitting on the lawn watching the spectacle of the ambulance taking Cecilia Lisbon to the hospital, the film links several events directly to the boys right away. The scenes of Paul Baldino recounting his (false?) story of finding Cecilia, Dominic Palazzollo jumping into the bushes, and, most significantly, the rec room party which presages Cecilia's successful suicide attempt are all situated with the boys either present, directly within frame, or from the expected vantage point of the boys watching. All of these events occur early in the film, although, it should be noted that not all the initial scenes are linked to the boys. Later in the film, there are scenes of the boys together examining the artifacts, such as Cecilia's diary, connected to the Lisbon girls and of the boys directly interacting with the girls through playing records over the phone to each other. Other scenes, such as the boys seeing the girls in the travel catalogs, seem to be fantasies offered by one or more of the boys. Therefore, there is a consistent thread of scenes which seems to connect the action directly with the group of teenage boys. The narrator is just one of these boys grown up. Coppola, of course, strategically never identifies which of the teen boys is telling the story.

Crucially, there are a substantial number of scenes that cannot be attributed, either directly or indirectly, to the boys. After being seduced and abandoned by Trip, there is a lengthy scene of Lux waking up alone on the football field. She makes her way home by cab, and her distraught parents meet her on the doorstep. The boys would have no way of knowing what transpired that night—only Lux and Trip would know about the lovemaking that night, while only Lux would recall how she woke up and made her way home. Scenes of reporter Lydia Perl interviewing the girls and of the neighbors commenting at various times on the action also do not appear to be the perspective of the boys either.

The viewer discovers that the film's allegiance to the boys fails to account for all the narrational strategies. In fact, Coppola moves between five different perspectives or storytelling modes: personal memory, collective memory, 'exhibits,' interviews, and neighborhood folklore. Personal memory consists of scenes with one or more of the teen boys present. These scenes can be attributed directly to the memory of one or more of our narrators. Collective memory involves those scenes in which the boys express an agreed upon 'conclusion' from their youth. As an example, the narrator comments that 'all the dumbest boys' dated Lux. The clips following of 'dumb' boys making lewd comments about Lux seem to be motivated by the group rather than by any one of the boys individually. 'Exhibits' are the artifacts linked to the Lisbon sisters, used to motivate the story and its development. Coppola treats these exhibits with less reverence than the Eugenides novel, although several are included in the film. Cecilia's diary, discovered by the boys, inspires an array of images from Lux stroking the whale, hula dancing and playing with the sparklers. The interviews include both the quick shots of Lux's suitors and the more extended direct-to-camera talks, like the adult Trip Fontaine discussing his memories of Lux. Neighborhood folklore addresses all those moments that create a sense of the suburban neighborhood. Certainly, the establishing shots of the neighborhood yards, barbeques and outdoor activity place the Lisbon story in a larger social context. These outdoor shots are also augmented by brief glimpses, unanchored in the film, of the neighbors commenting on the Lisbon family. These shots do not have the same gravitas as the extended interview of the middle-aged Trip Fontaine. They are, instead, very brief sound bites populating the film to give it texture and depth.

Although Coppola does generally stay close to the novel's outline, these narrational strategies differ in a few significant ways from the book. Eugenides' narrators rely much more heavily on collecting the exhibits which

they describe as their 'strange curatorship.' As one entry describes a typical find, 'We have a few documents from the time (Exhibits #13–15)—
Therese's chemistry write-ups, Bonnie's history paper on Simone Weil,
Lux's frequent forged excuses from phys. ed' (Eugenides 1993: 97). The
novel includes references to medical diagnoses of the girls, photos of the
home, prom pictures, newspaper articles, coroners' reports, and many other
'relevant' facts connected to the Lisbons. In a playful, postmodern manner,
Eugenides proliferates these exhibits, almost as if they were clues for the
Lisbon suicides. Curation of the exhibits is a problem; as the boys admit,
'We've tried to arrange the photographs chronologically, though the passage of so many years has made it difficult' (1993: 2–3). The organization of
the exhibits is haphazard, as would be expected if 15-year-olds had been in
charge of them. Tellingly, Eugenides does not include any of the exhibits in
an appendix. The mystery in the novel is surrounded by lots of half-recalled
artifacts which receive almost no analysis from the boys. By the end of
the book, the narrator obliquely comments, 'all of it is going,' referring
to the five suitcases containing the Lisbon artifacts. 'We haven't kept our
tomb sufficiently airtight, and our sacred objects are perishing' (1993: 241)
explains the narrator.

The novel also includes several references to interviews with the characters at some point after the deaths of the girls. Coppola's film includes only
one: the middle-aged Trip Fontaine talking to an unspecified interviewer
from his stint in rehab. Eugenides' novel has a sustained strategy of these
ex-post interviews. Some of these later interviews are with characters dramatized in the film: Mr. Lisbon, Mrs. Lisbon, Father Moody, Lydia Perl,
the journalist, and Dr. Hornicker, the psychiatrist. There are, however, several other interviews in the book conducted years after the Lisbon deaths,
including Dr. Becker, the orthodontist; Muffie Perry, a Lisbon school
friend; and Lema Crawford, the Lisbon grandmother. Together with those
characters that appear in the film, these interviews constitute another layer
of information and discovery in the book. Some of these interviews do, in
fact, shed light on the case of the Lisbon girls. Muffie Perry recounts experiences interacting with the school therapist, including visits to the therapist
by the Lisbon girls. With the sole exception of middle-aged Trip, all these
interviews are missing from Coppola's film.

A Confusion of Perspectives

Coppola's narrational modes largely elide the 'years later' interview strategy
so important to Eugenides. Shifting between the five narrational storytelling modes, Coppola, in fact, presents an even more complicated structure
than the novel. Media scholars have been intrigued and frustrated by this
model of storytelling. Academic criticism on this storytelling has focused

on the influences that derail or confound conventional explanation or narrative development. Anna Backman Rogers emphasizes the impact of time on the construction of the narrative. For Rogers, the gap of years makes the storytelling fallible and suspect: 'Similarly, with *The Virgin Suicides*, the past (as the pure force of time) acts as a power that confounds any attempt to form an explanation for the tragedy in the present moment' (2012: 151). Rogers sees the film as including 'false memories,' manufactured by the boys, as a key means of storytelling. The shots of Lux touching the whale from the boat are examples of these imagined scenes to which the boys do not have any direct contact. For Rogers, this strategy leaves the boys and, more importantly, the film's viewers with a 'complete void of understanding' in constructing the story of the Lisbon girls (156).

For Debra Shostak, the issue of the film's narration is more focused on perspective rather than the gap in time. Shostak describes how the issue of perspective is key to the film, but is complicated by Coppola: 'Coppola's film, on the contrary, conveys an inconsistent viewpoint because of the multiple ways the camera's positioning may be construed' (2013: 192). Shostak argues that the film tends to place the viewer in the position of the voyeuristic boys. This perspective admittedly is definitely suspect. To extrapolate from this premise, it is worth considering how even the film's tone is impacted by this positioning. If we accept that the film is 'told' by the middle-aged men looking back on their youth, several scenes appear to be tonally inconsistent with 'reality.' They are, in fact, told in hyperbolic terms to maximize the fun and vivid quality of the anecdote. Whether this is 'false memory' or an actively constructed falsehood by the narrators is debatable. Several scenes in the film strain credulity through touches or elements that 'make for a good story' but are, nonetheless, difficult to believe. The examples range from small incidental details to entire scenes. Consider, for instance, the scene of the neighborhood men pulling the Lisbon fence from the yard after Cecilia has committed suicide by leaping onto it. The scene plays out as a spectacle, with much of the neighborhood in attendance. Coppola even includes one of the wives holding a tray of drinks while the men are working. The bevy of neighbors and the idea of 'catering' seem more like the product of an overactive teen imagination—or, to use Rogers' term, a false memory. Similarly, the TV report on Rannie, the teen who made a rat poison pie that killed her grandmother, also is barely credible (would the family really allow her to appear on camera in this way?). Coppola cuts the report to a deadpan suburban matron watching TV with a cocktail in hand. The connection between these two shots (the Rannie report and the bored and soused matron) makes the scene a gag, giving humor to the story that it would not otherwise possess. It is also the kind of 'low humor' that fits the mind of a teen boy rather than an adult. Filtering through the perspective of the boys impacts the film at many points.

Other scenes are presented in a straightforward manner as if believed entirely by the boys. Think about the early meeting with Paul Baldino, the mobster's son, who explains how he discovered Cecilia's suicide attempt. Baldino's father has an underground network connecting the neighborhood homes through the sewer. Even more astonishing is the claim that this network is accessed through the family BBQ in the front yard. Baldino's story is told without question and without doubt. The boys implicitly endorse this bizarre—and highly unlikely—anecdote. The scene shows an audience member that, even while presented plainly, action in the movie must be seen as understood through the consciousness of the teen boys, now middle-aged men. Caveat emptor is the rule for *The Virgin Suicides* viewer.

Perspective is also blurred since identities are conflated among both the boys and the girls. While there is a solo male narrator, the neighborhood boys receive little differentiation from each other. Their names are only used intermittently, and Coppola encourages the viewers to think of the boys as a collective rather than as individuals. Consequently, the viewer never connects strongly with any of the male teens. Their appearances are just too fleeting. With the Lisbon sisters, the story is slightly more complicated. The youngest, Cecilia, is separated from the sisters since she commits suicide early in the film. Afterwards, Cecilia is demonized by the neighbors as a 'kook,' and placed aside from the other Lisbon girls. Of the four remaining sisters, three (Bonnie/Therese/Mary) are treated as a group. As Shostak notes, 14-year-old Lux is treated as the dominant sister by the boys (2013: 186). So, while it is inaccurate to state that the identities of the Lisbon girls are blurred, three of the sisters are virtually indistinguishable.

Lux drives much of the narrative in both novel and film. Not coincidentally, Lux is also the character most heavily sexualized in the story. While the boys talk about the Lisbon sisters, they offer specific details and anecdotes almost entirely based around Lux. Lux's flirtation and relationship with Trip Fontaine motivates most of the subsequent action, including the parents grounding all the daughters and taking them out of school. Coppola opens the film with a bored Lux (Kirsten Dunst) sucking on a red candy (see Figure 3.2) and eventually just walking out of the frame.

The opening creates a parallel between Lux and Vladimir Nabokov's *Lolita*. Indeed, Lux is seen as possessing a healthy sexual appetite throughout the film. Most of the time, we witness this in a flirtation manner but eventually this does lead to Lux consummating her relationships after the crackdown by the parents. Coppola makes a distinct shift in the portrayal of Lux's sexuality compared to the book. Eugenides paints a much more vivid history of her sexual activity. Coppola softens this considerably. The film moves toward more of a romantic idealization of Lux's sexuality unlike the more graphic and upsetting details present in the novel. After her assignations on

Figure 3.2 Lux's introduction, the female teen sucking a candy pop

the roof of the home, Lux fakes the symptoms of a ruptured appendix and is transported by ambulance to the hospital. Once there, she reveals to the doctor that she might be pregnant. Curiously, the doctor agrees not to tell the Lisbon parents about this potential. The boys pay Ms. Angelica Turnette, a hospital clerical worker, for the case file of Lux' admission. The results are sobering: "'The pregnancy test was negative, but it was clear she was sexually active,' Ms. Turnette told us. 'She had HPV [human papilloma virus, a precursor to genital warts]. The more partners you have, the more HPV. It's that simple'" (Eugenides 1993: 150). Lux's encounters with the various boys on the rooftop are also cut substantially in the film. While the book recounts these liaisons in detail, the film limits the scenes to just a few seconds of screen time. In addition, while Eugenides makes reference to the boys masturbating to the images and memories of the Lisbon girls, this anecdote is elided by Coppola. The director deletes the more graphic and sordid aspects of the sexuality in the book. What remains in the film is the temptress Lux, largely without the more explicit details of her sexual history.

The Enigma Reconsidered: Sexuality, Suicide & Bearing Witness

The viewer centers attention then on Lux and her three beautiful, but undifferentiated, sisters. The youngest is typed as a 'kook,' unstable and drawn to dark experiences. Coppola creates a vision of female sexuality that is compelling for the boys and, indeed, for viewers of the film. Lux is the focal point, representing a strong female sexuality, with an open and warm quality that makes her beauty even more alluring. The three other sisters are the beautiful 'virgins,' chaste but still friendly and inviting to the boys (evidence how quickly they bond with the boys during the group date to the prom). *The Virgin Suicides* therefore is not so much a mystery about the 'whys' of suicide, but rather a curious meditation on female sexuality. Given that the narrators are teenage boys, this meditation quickly becomes an obsession. Coppola slyly telegraphs this throughout the film. In the most obvious example, she cuts from a scene of math teacher Mr. Lisbon explaining the difference between 'union' and 'intersection' with shots to Lux flirting with a boy on the lawn outside the classroom. The sexual 'intersection' powering the film is made explicit through this connection.

The boys' fascination with the Lisbon girls leads to the climactic scene when the boys arrive at the Lisbon household late one night. The boys' expectation is that the girls will want to escape on a road trip. This is, however, just a conjecture that they somehow believe strongly. Lux meets the group of four boys, and openly flirts with Chase, unbuckling his belt as she asks him about riding shotgun during their road trip. She exits the house to get the car ready, and the boys are left in the rec room to wait for the sisters. Soon they start to explore the house. As Chase says, 'These girls make me crazy. If I could just feel one of them up just once,' he collides with Bonnie hanging from the ceiling. The boys hastily retreat, with the narrator explaining how the other girls also committed suicide. The scene links the fascination with female sexuality and death in a direct manner. Coppola and Eugenides confound the search for psychological or personal motivation behind the suicides. They shift the argument to the intersection of youthful sexuality and death instead.

The path of the film shifts at this climax. Michelle Aaron astutely labels this dynamic in *The Virgin Suicides* as a fascination with 'necromanticism.' Aaron claims that the cinema is a problematic space to engage necromanticism: 'It is mainstream cinema's emphasis not just on happy endings but also on the strengthening of certain notions of the self that tends to make it shy from the more morbid and nihilistic versions of self-endangerment' (2014: 72). Aaron suggests that the boys remain 'eternally haunted' by the experience of encountering the girls since their obsession with them is so overdetermined (78–79). This analysis is useful since it redirects the argument away from the conventional model of mystery toward more of a social explanation for the book and film. Aaron pushes the Lisbon tale away from the personal tale of the Lisbon tragedy through suggesting that the film is more about 'Western Culture's necromantic obsession with women'(80).

Addressing the enigma more broadly, the story fits clearly in the sociological literature on suicide and causal social factors. Writing in 1897, Emile Durkheim isolated a range of social factors, including family structure, religion and changes in class position, that provide a key context for belonging and that can lead, given a set of social determinants, to suicide. Durkheim labels 'egotistical suicide' as the most widespread form: 'The individual no longer wishes to live, because he is no longer attached to the only intermediary between himself and reality, which is society' (2006: 396). Separating the Lisbon girls from the friends and school in the family 'lockdown' at home represents just this kind of isolation from society. To follow Durkheim, this drastic measure of social isolation would be significant as a causal factor. Sociologists have tended to reinforce this claim over the years, presenting the inclusion of a person into a larger social group as central to healthy development. As evidence of this relationship, Justin Denney and Jay Teachman link both a sense of belonging and a connection to a collective moral life to a lower suicide risk (Denney and Teachman 2010: 210). Empirical evidence appears to favor this model: Jessica Portner, writing in 2001, cites 'relative social isolation' of teens in western US states as one key reason for higher teen suicide compared to the populous New England region of the USA (2001: 4). With social connections stripped from the Lisbon girls, it would suggest a heightened suicide risk for the girls.

Interestingly, Durkheim also addresses mass suicide; as he states, 'It is not to be doubted that the idea of suicide is spread by contagion' (2006: 124). Durkheim argues for a 'collective resolve' or a social consensus as the key factor in multiple suicides. In popular culture, the notion of a suicide pact can be seen as a romantic notion as much as a fatalistic one. Stacie Ramey's young adult novel *The Sister Pact* (2015) offers such a scenario through exploring the bond between two young sisters who vow to be together always, in life and in death. Coppola and Eugenides draw directly on this notion of a suicide pact or a social consensus spreading loss throughout the film. Death and illness are linked several times through the fear of a transmission of both. The disease of the dying elms in the neighborhood, the asphyxiation prom party, and the news reports on the trend for suicide all speak to the concept that suicide can be spread through direct contact and association with those already afflicted. This contagion model only furthers the mystery of suicide, making the cause more impersonal and distant. So, one of the key groundbreaking figures in sociology sketched the path for the Lisbon girls more than a century ago. Character psychology is trumped by social factors and determinants as the rationale for the mass suicides.

Elevating the inquiry to the realm of sociology leads to another path altogether. Eugenides has stated that the book is really about the survivors of the Lisbon tragedy rather than about the girls or their motives (Schiff 2006: 114).

Perhaps the central enigma of the film is not the causal factors leading to the suicide, but rather the strategies and means that others use to manage the suicides after the fact. The mystery is not about the reasons for the suicide, but rather the fascination with the event. In this way, the film is inverted: despite the title, the film is really centered on the boys, not the Lisbon girls. The enigma becomes why the boys are so captured by the event and the means through which they are able to process the tragedy over the years.

In effect, the boys have experienced trauma directly through being witnesses to the Lisbon girls. The girls have implicated the neighborhood boys in the event, perhaps to bear witness to their deaths or to the injustices that they were forced to live under. Regardless of the motive, the boys are placed in the position as 'listeners' to the victims. A key part of the psychological process related to bearing witness to trauma is the ability of the witnesses to narrate the witnessing process itself. Debra Jackson describes this function in these terms: 'Not only does the witness assist the survivors in constructing their self-narrative, but the survivor constructs her own self-narrative as an agent of change. Through witnessing trauma, the status of the victims is changed from object to subject of a narrative, and through critical self-refection, the listener develops into a more empathetic and responsible listener' (2016: 225). The narration of the film, therefore, can be seen as an attempt by the grown men to 'bear witness' to the scarring events of their youth. By bearing witness, the boys are able to cope with the events, translating them into a loose narrative rather than dealing with the messiness of reality and the unexplained.

Looking at the film through this prism does explain both the shift in narrational modes and some of the more curious gaps or lapses in the storytelling. The film is actually the product of the adult narrator sharing the story at, as previously noted, a cocktail party or a business lunch. As the years have progressed, only the 'highlights' or most vivid memories remain. This structure also explains why Eugenides is fond of thinking of the title as 'tabloid'; tabloid stories always grab the most interest through sensationalism and hyperbole. This results in Coppola's film having the strange gags (e.g., the deadpan look of the drunk matron to the TV report) and the larger-than-life representations (e.g., the idolization of Trip Fontaine for being the most successful suitor of Lux). Returning to the five narrational modes (personal memory, collective memory, 'exhibits,' interviews, neighborhood folklore) in the film, considering the film as 'bearing witness' assumes that the two autonomous modes (the interviews and the neighborhood gossip) are, in fact, associated with the middle-aged men as well. Certainly, this explanation pushes the film closer to the structure of the book in which the men interview several of the characters years later, not just Trip. Seeing the film as bearing witness also explains the narrative device of 'laddering up' the

Lisbon suicides to account for the demise or decline of the larger issues (decline of the neighborhood, the auto industry) mentioned by the narrator. The narrator is simply framing his 'case study' in a larger context to make the story even more compelling and noteworthy. In this mode, the film echoes *Bad Timing: A Sensual Obsession* through an unreliable, and often misleading, narrator. With the central enigma or mystery explicated but never solved, deliberately, Coppola's film also echoes both *L'Avventura* and *Picnic at Hanging Rock*.

Thinking of the film as bearing witness also reinforces the basic premise against the Laura Mulvey scenario of visual pleasure (1975: 6–18). If 'sadism demands a story,' the boys/men enact their own story—exaggerated, imagined and revised—according to their own perception (14). Further, the gender imbalance crucial to the Mulvey model is replicated perfectly: the boys/men are the narrators, and the girls are presented, almost entirely, as 'to be looked at' or desired. The agency of the girls within the film is limited entirely by the means of storytelling. The narrational devices bolster the separation of the sexes, with the Lisbon girls either mute or as the embodiment of the male narrator's fantasy. Like so much of classical Hollywood cinema, *The Virgin Suicides* illustrates clearly that the voyeurism and fetishization structure the narrative and the viewer's entry into the film. In this way, despite the originality of the narrational modes, *The Virgin Suicides* absolutely reinforces traditional gender roles and stereotypes.

Toward the end of the novel, the narrator reviews theories associated with the Lisbon suicide, including Dr. Hornicker's theory of Post-Traumatic Stress Disorder and Lydia Perl's claim of an 'esoteric ritual of self-sacrifice.' These explanations, as well as others, are elided by Coppola. Coppola is more insistent on leaving the film open-ended, with the mystery unreconciled. Although the case is never reconciled, as in the novel, events after the mass suicide tend to undercut the enigma of the mass suicide. For instance, the debutante ball with the theme of asphyxiation, including gas masks and a drunk partygoer screaming, 'I'm a teenager, I've got problems,' seems to satirize the multiple deaths for a humorous impact. The scene diminishes the emotional impact of the deaths, placing them into a strange black comic perspective.

Returning to the notion of bearing witness, the narrator might be interested in processing the events and all the connections, but the effort never leads to a conclusion. In this way, Coppola respects the fascination created by intersecting female sexuality and death for the narrator. The potency of this connection remains for the boys (now men). To find answers to the Lisbon deaths, or even to posit reasonable hypotheses, would numb the extraordinary fascination with sex/death at the core of the film. One of the last images in the film is the four friends saluting the Lisbon home with a raised lighter. The gesture is juvenile, more appropriate to a rock concert encore than to remembering the girls. The lighter in the air is perfect though as a mark of how the boys now men have filtered the information (haphazardly, incoherently). Like *L'Avventura* and *Picnic at Hanging Rock*, the 'mystery' cannot be solved. Like *Bad Timing*, perspective, memory and control all impact the storytelling to a great degree. Consequently, the 'answers' will never be found and the story of sexuality and demise continues to haunt them—and unsuspecting moviegoers expecting a mystery but finding so much more.

Note

1. The salient example of this strategy is the flashback of Alex and Milena having sex on the staircase. Netusil is cut into the action, with the detective even licking his lips in delight while watching the couple.

4   Music, Storytelling and Young Love

During the decade between her appearance in *The Godfather Part III* and her directorial debut, Sofia Coppola engaged in a wide variety of artistic and creative pursuits. Many of these endeavors were connected to the world of music. Coppola appeared in music videos for, among others, The Black Crowes, Madonna, Sonic Youth and The Chemical Brothers. At the same time, Sofia's brother Roman was beginning to become a recognized director of innovative and bold music videos, for such bands as Green Day, Daft Punk, and especially Fatboy Slim's memorable Christopher Walken dancing opus, 'Gangster Trippin'' (1998).[1] In 1998, Roman directed the video for the hit song, 'Sexy Boy,' from Air's *Moon Safari* album. Given this activity and the connections, it is hardly surprising that Sofia's debut feature draws heavily on the power of music to create meaning and to elicit emotion from the viewer. While Eugenides' novel includes some fleeting references to music, Coppola's musical choices help to create an identity for the project as separate from the novel. The narrative line remains similar in outline, while the aural and visual choices made by Coppola become defining. In this way, the music becomes a key element in the film's style.

The Virgin Suicides operates on a dual register in its use of music, via French electronic band Air's evocative score and soundtrack album, and also a carefully selected set of 1970s pop, folk and rock songs. The choices made in both of these musical forms are deceptive. At first glance, the music may seem incidental and lacking in a core connection to the drama. The brief soundtrack appearances of both the Air score and the existing 1970s songs belie their importance to the film. Even in their brevity, the musical accompaniment builds the emotion of the drama and the creation of her cinematic 'environment' in clear ways. Closer analysis, however, illustrates that Coppola is, in fact, also very strategic in her choices for both of these musical worlds. Through understanding how music operates in the film, the viewer can appreciate a deeper social and cultural context in *The Virgin Suicides* world.

The Unbearable Lightness of Air

Coppola commissioned the French electronic duo Air (Jean-Benoit Dunckel and Nicolas Godin) to construct the film's soundtrack. Their 1998 debut album, *Moon Safari*, was heavily indebted to aspects of the 1970s 'analog sound' through the use of Moog synthesizers and valve amplifiers. Linking back to the work of Jean-Michel Jarre in the 1970s, the music of Air was foundational in several respects. Like Etienne de Crecy and Daft Punk, Air's music became part of a movement tagged 'French Touch,' a set of ambient and electronic musical artists (Anon 2012). Apart from the electronic focus, the French Touch music generally occupies a unique space between France and America. While French in origin, the lyrics were usually sung in English. Often the lyrics were either just a few words or a slogan, repeated without expression or dramatic inflection. Rather than use the music to express an emotion or to work through a feeling, the French Touch music instead seemed to privilege an exhaustion of meaning.[2] The music created a postmodern pastiche of pop styles set to a minimal electronic beat. As would be expected, the club scene of the mid- to late-1990s gravitated toward this musical genre.

The Virgin Suicides was made in the late 1990s describing a Michigan town in the mid-1970s. This discrepancy also suggests a dislocation that matches with the French Touch music. Thinking about the score in terms of this temporal dislocation adds another dimension. On the one hand, Air's music invokes the electronic soundtracks of other films from the 1970s and beyond. Tangerine Dream (*Sorcerer* (William Friedkin, 1977), *Thief* (Michael Mann, 1981), *Risky Business* (Paul Brickman, 1983)) and Giorgio Moroder (*Midnight Express* (Alan Parker, 1978), *American Gigolo* (Paul Schrader, 1980), *Cat People* (Paul Schrader, 1982)) are the most distinctive examples of this musical scoring: elegant, sleek and minimal in design. Coppola's use of the Air score achieves this double focus, recalling the 1970s electronic soundtracks in the context of the French Touch music of the 1990s. In this way, the film recalls these classic scores, setting *The Virgin Suicides* in a specific time and place when electronic soundtracks were the most 'cutting edge.' The high water mark, commercially and aesthetically, for these soundtracks was Vangelis' score for *Chariots of Fire* (Hugh Hudson, 1981), which reached #1 on the Billboard charts.

Another 1970s musical trope is also raised by Coppola: the era of the easy listening record. As Keir Keightley recounts, in post-war America, suburban tastes skewed to 'easy listening,' or to music that required little in terms of attention or engagement. These records included 'mood music' for listeners to augment their desired emotions and, to use Keightley's term, MOR (middle-of-the-road) music. MOR music included instrumental recordings or standards, hit songs, and popular non-rock vocals (Keightley 2008: 309–335). MOR music offered a stripped-down version of contemporary and perennial hit music, sanitized by adhering just to the instrumental line and to the softer non-rock beats. Ray Conniff, Roger Miller, Andre Kostelanetz, and Bert Kaempfert gained significant popularity for this music in the 60s and 70s. Of course, by the early 1970s, this music was pitted against rock, in particular, and even contemporary pop music. Detractors referred to the MOR music as 'muzak' to be played in retail spaces and elevators. Air's score could be seen as MOR music of the 1970s. There are certainly overlaps and parallels between them: simple themes, strictly instrumental, and, until the credits, omitting the original song reference. Instead, the theme 'Playground Love' is used to create a number of the other instrumental tracks earlier in the film. As such, in the culture wars of the Lisbon family, Air's soundtrack would appeal to Mr. and Mrs. Lisbon whose strict conservatism, middle age, and middle class taste all align with the MOR music.

Air's score, therefore, evokes the past through recalling the electronic music scores and retaining a simplicity associated with the MOR artists of that era. The displacement in time, however, makes the Air score distinctive. The score is not simply a pastiche or an empty attempt at recreating a 'lost' form. Instead, given Air's French Touch origins, the score becomes refracted through this genre of ambient music. Unusual phrasing, blank emotion, and repetitive chords take the music into another realm where the comfort and safety of MOR no longer apply. These musical choices align the soundtrack with the cinematic narrative. The story of *The Virgin Suicides* continually slips away, as the clues and evidence offer little insight into the tragedy of the Lisbon suicides. The music, like Coppola's film overall, bolsters this process by suggesting a mood of discomfort and anxiety through the temporal and musical dislocations.

Coppola uses Air's music sparingly and strategically in the film. In particular, Coppola is very aware of the dramatic potential for music followed abruptly by silence. This feels like the aural equivalent of a jump cut. The viewer is lulled by the hypnotic score only to be thrown back into the harsh narrative development. In the opening scenes, the tranquil shots of the neighborhood and the sunlight through the trees matched with the instrumental score drops suddenly with the narration 'Cecilia was the first to go' and a shot of the bathroom with Cecilia's suicide attempt. The shot of Cecilia lying in the bathtub is followed by reactions from the neighbors as she is taken away by the ambulance. As soon as the film cuts to the neighbors, the instrumental track continues. The 'shock' of Cecilia's suicide attempt halts the music, as well as the tranquil mood and atmosphere. Similarly, when student Peter Lisson uses the girls' bathroom in the Lisbon home, the track

('Bathroom Girl') is amplified as he sensually explores the world of their perfumes, lipstick and cosmetics. Air's music track is cut abruptly as Lux knocks on the door: Peter's reverie is broken and so is the accompanying music. Coppola therefore offers another 'shock cut' using the music and then silence as a way to jolt the audience back to reality. Coppola effectively integrates the Air soundtrack with the mise-en-scène and mood of the film. The violence and harsh realities of the suicides are antithetical to this atmosphere.

The centerpiece of Air's score is the song 'Playground Love' which is used in its entirety over the end credits of the film. At several points earlier, Air employ the instrumental refrain and a piano accompaniment of 'Playground Love' as incidental music. The audience is therefore familiar with the instrumental version before hearing the full song over the credits. The song was actually commissioned by music supervisor Brian Reitzell after the score was completed. Consequently, the echoes to the pre-existing tracks make sense. Vocals on 'Playground Love' are by Gordon Tracks, a pseudonym of Thomas Mars (and eventual husband to Sofia Coppola) from the band Phoenix. Each musical component—synthesizer, piano, strings, saxophone—are added one-by-one so the basic structure and melody of the song are always present. The track is slow, very deliberately paced in a way that suggests a vague melancholy or lethargy. Mars' vocals, in French Touch, seemed drained of emotion. The lyrics become almost a recitation rather than a vocal accompaniment. Again, echoes of easy listening come to mind, as well as perhaps a drug or alcohol induced teenage ennui.

The title 'Playground Love' perfectly captures the tension between innocence and experience crucial to so much of the film. Initially, it may seem as if the title refers to a young, prepubescent affection; only schoolchildren use a playground and love would then be entirely innocuous. The opening lyrics ('I'm a high school lover, and you're my favorite flavor/Love is all, all my soul/ You're my playground love') shift the context to high school when 'love' can have a much greater charge and more serious consequences. So, the song is pitched in the area between the young and old, innocence and experience. The remainder of Air's song offers several archetypes of teen love: 'my hands are shaking'; 'I'm on fire'; 'you're the piece of gold'; 'anytime, anywhere.' The song fails to carry a narrative line. It is composed, instead, of a few images conjuring passion and obsession among teenagers. Lines are unconnected, and the listener is left with discrete images and feelings, nothing more.

The theme song confounds expectations. It is neither a melancholy theme on loss nor a tale of unrequited love. The deliberate pacing, electronic instrumentation, and prosaic singing suggest something else entirely. With *Blue Velvet* (1986), David Lynch uses banal pop songs from the 1950s to expose the underbelly of small town suburban life in the 1980s. Sucking on nitrous oxide, Frank Booth (Dennis Hopper) recites the 'In Dreams' lyrics ('A candy-colored clown they call the sandman/Tiptoes to my room every night/Just to sprinkle stardust and to whisper/'Go to sleep. Everything is all right') to Roy Orbison's classic song as he brutalizes and humiliates Jeffrey (Kyle MacLachlan). At the same time, a middle-aged go-go dancer from the 1960s gyrates slowly on top of Frank's car. Lynch forces the viewer to consider the emptiest of pop sentiment against a context of sadism, drug abuse and sexual violence. Context shifts the bland lyrics on love and obsession into a different uncomfortable space for viewers to reconsider the original song. While 'Playground Love' does not benefit from the nostalgic recall of *Blue Velvet*'s 'In Dreams,' there are certainly parallels. The lethargic tempo, bland enunciation, and disconnected images question the parameters of the typical teen love song. 'Playground Love' may seem like soft rock or pop of the 1970s, but the musical choices undo our expectations and orientations of these simple love songs. Instead, the viewer is left to contemplate the curious components of the song's imagery (e.g., shaking hands, favorite flavor, the piece of gold, extra time on the ground). Of course, occurring over the end credits, the song also must be considered in the context of the film's action: the playground love against the multiple suicides and obsessed middle-aged men.

Only four of the thirteen Air tracks in the movie soundtrack are represented in the film. With Air's score limited to brief excerpts and the end credits, the soundtrack album presents another useful entry point to the film. Acclaimed by music critics and popular with listeners, Air's soundtrack was actually just one of the albums released in conjunction with the film. Another album included pre-existing pop, folk and rock songs from the 1970s used as incidental music in the film. The Air soundtrack offers a more comprehensive view of the brief themes in the film. Jean-Benoit Dunckel of Air sums up the creative process leading to this design: 'At the beginning, we really were watching the movie and we were trying to synchronize the music with the movie, all the scenes. At the end, during the mixing, we forgot about the movie, and we turned the thing into songs, thinking of music that you could listen to by yourself, alone' (Rachel 2015). Tonally, the individual music tracks fit together perfectly, as critic Jim Harrington refers to them as just 'one gloriously sad suite' (2006: 861). Some tracks start with the 'Playground Love' theme and then morph it with a somewhat different emphasis: 'Highschool Lover' (among the first words of 'Playground Love') presents a more somber view of the theme augmented with a simple (high school?) piano; church organs give 'Bathroom Girl' a majestic tone; keyboard heavy 'Cemetary Party' becomes more like a march than a quiet, reflective pop song. As Harrington suggests, the tracks, in total, are united in their somber, synth approach to the theme of loss (ibid.). In conjunction with the film, Air's soundtrack deepens Coppola's created world; in effect, the soundtrack is inspired by the film and is tonally and thematically consistent.

Not all of Air's tracks develop from their main theme. There are also instances of Air expanding and extending the film through their choice of music. Air's Jean-Benoit Dunckel explains that the soundtrack was guided by a larger theme than just the narrative line: 'I think the real spirit of the soundtrack is this fascination with death and the fascination with having your spirit floating when you die and how you suddenly feel free and liberated from earth, from all you are and the adult's world that you actually hate' (quoted in Jones 2015). In 'Suicide Underground,' a vibraphone is used to inflect the narration into an even deeper, more sinister note. With several selected narrations—from the opening of the demise of the neighborhood to listing the girls' ages and recounting the shutdown of the house—the story of *The Virgin Suicides* is offered, Cliff Notes style, to the listener. Against the augmented voice-over, the story becomes more horrific. The trajectory is summed up quickly and the narrator sounds possessed so that listeners must consider the story in the framework of a nightmare or horror story.

The most audacious track, 'The Word "Hurricane,"' is centered on the scene of Trip flirting with Lux during the class screening of the science documentary. Against the documentary's soundtrack, Trip tells Lux he will ask her out, and she responds laughingly, 'fat chance.' He persists, and she demurely smiles and acts slightly smitten. The attention in the scene is directly to the flirtation and the possibility that Lux is finally warming up to Trip as a suitor. The audio of the documentary explains how warm and cold air come together to produce the hurricane. The parallel to the male/female sexual tension is obvious. The connection between the science documentary and the flirtation between the characters makes for a funny second layer of meaning in the scene. Air's 'The Word "Hurricane"' inverts the equation in an interesting way. Starting with a synth matched to a heavenly choir, the track juxtaposes the documentary soundtrack on the formation of a hurricane with sounds of teen passion. In the film, the scene is played lightly with little connection between the dramatic action of the couple and the documentary soundtrack. The song, in making the connection much more explicit, pushes the action into a hyperbolic state. The song reflects on the scene, making it more tabloid, dirtier and sexier than the film. Air forces a reconsideration of the simple scene, creating a satirical version of teen passion rather than the straightforward presentation in the film. In this way, the Air soundtrack adds a way to expand the potential meanings from the cinematic text. Interestingly, taking the scene into more of a tabloid context draws the film actually closer to the grittier, unvarnished world presented by Jeffrey Eugenides in his novel.

Music, Gender and Space in *The Virgin Suicides*

The Air soundtrack is augmented with a variety of 1970s pop, folk and rock songs designed to be evocative of the period and to comment on the action. This selection of 'classic' music in the film is particularly significant since music is so formative to teenagers. Coppola uses music to give texture to characters who are largely undefined in other ways. Music becomes a means to understand the Lisbon girls as a group. Their drives, feelings and emotions are rarely expressed directly. Instead, music is used as a substitute to help the viewer understand the girls more fully.

In this way, Coppola is using music as a kind of badge, a way to express and release emotion and to define ourselves in society (Frith 2007: 264). Music is a particularly powerful force for the teenager since it can be used a way to express both individual identity and group identity. In post-World War II America, these forces for identity formation were shaped within the larger market of the American teenager (Osgerby 2008: 27–58). Like other mass-mediated items, music's power was also impacted by the larger commercial sphere. Regardless, music helps to construct, negotiate and modify both types of identity formation. For the adolescent, music occupies a special place in their development by helping to meet emotional needs, distracting them from boredom, and relieving tension and stress (Campbell et al. 2007: 220–236). Theorist Jacques Attali makes an even bolder claim for the role. Attali contends that music is, in fact, transformative: 'Music has the explicit function of reassuring. The whole of musicology analyzes music as the organization of controlled panic, the transformation of anxiety into joy, and of dissonance into harmony' (1985: 27). Understanding that Attali has raised the stakes on the function of music, the hypothesis is nevertheless that music—especially for the adolescent—occupies a central part in crafting personal image, identity and aspirations.

As with much of the mass media, music has been coded by gender in multiple ways. In terms of the apparatus, Keir Keightley builds the case that audio technology has been gendered as masculine by the 1950s (1996: 149–177). By genre, Tim Anderson suggests that rock has been associated with the masculine, while pop music is linked to the feminine (2013: 70). Pamela Robertson Wojcik uses the film *Diner* (Barry Levinson, 1982) to demonstrate how the culture of record collecting is marked as masculine, while the record player is branded as female only when considered as part of the domestic space (2001: 433–454). *Diner*'s scene of Shreevie (Daniel Stern) arguing with Beth (Ellen Barkin) over miscataloging the records demon-strates how mastery over music and music collecting aligns strongly with the masculine. This is contrasted with Beth's simple pleasure of listening, which is tagged as feminine and marked as less important than the (male) process of collecting and cataloging. The coding of music and technology by gender also matches with Attali's model for how music operates in soci-ety. While transformative, music does, in fact, still serve a key function of simulating and affirming the accepted 'rules' of society. Gender roles and stereotypes fit into this system seamlessly.

The gender divisions over music and listening also play out in terms of physical space. Jeanne Steele and Jane D. Brown's 1995 study, 'Ado-lescent Room Culture: Studying Media in the Context of Everyday Life,' illustrates how teenagers use their rooms as a place to consume media, to create meanings from media and daily life, and to construct their own identities (1995: 551–576). Steele and Brown see media consumption as an active process in which individuals shape and transform media content as part of their identity formation. This is accomplished, in part, through the private space of their rooms. In this space, the teens can engage in many activities (watching television, talking to friends, listening to music) as part of their identity formation. Steele and Brown view the process as active, with the teens appropriating media for their own purposes. Media in the safe space of their own rooms can make a statement about identity and can allow for an examination of cultural values. In their ethnographic study, Steele and Brown evidence a marked distinction in the use of per-sonal (bedroom) space by gender: female teens use the media to reinforce existing beliefs in romantic love and fulfillment whereas males did not (570). Male teens tended to be more aspirational through media consump-tion, while female teens were interested in reinforcing their world view through the media usage.

This mapping of gender, space and music is reflected directly in Cop-pola's film. Music is linked to specific gendered spaces as a means to define the characters and their dramatic situation. The Lisbon sisters are facing the death of their youngest sister, the crackdown leaving them housebound, and the alienation of their friends and schoolmates. Given these factors, it is hardly surprising that music plays such a crucial role in both the novel and the film. Certainly music is used within the film to suggest a means of caring and support—and the absence of it as an impetus for depression and acting out. In one of the turning points in the film, Mrs. Lisbon, inspired by a church sermon, decides to burn Lux's record collection. Lux pleas with her mother to save individual records ('not Kiss! Not Aerosmith!') as Mrs. Lisbon tosses the albums into the fire. Consumed by the smoke from the burnt vinyl, Mrs. Lisbon opens the front door. The tyrannical mother looks like the keeper to the gates of hell as smoke cascades over her while she holds the remaining record collection. The Lisbon home is transformed into hell for Lux as her music is relinquished. For Lux, the possibility of aligning with the theatrics of Kiss or the hard rock lifestyle of Aerosmith are destroyed by her mother. The scene underlines the key role that music plays for the female adolescent, and the danger that occurs to identity formation if such a relationship is severed.

Lux's album burning is just one of several scenes using music in strategic ways to tell the Lisbon story. The genre of music and the specific songs connect with types of spaces in the film. Space is also imagined in very particular ways in *The Virgin Suicides*. Kohei Usuda argues that Coppola tends to use claustrophobic spaces in her films to isolate her characters and limit their interactions with others (2008: 54–57). Indeed, the spaces used by Coppola in *The Virgin Suicides* are precisely defined and sometimes constricting for the characters. They are also matched with specific music and music genres. In terms of spaces, the film configures a family space, a shared teen space, and then space by gender (male/female). The girls' space is linked both with Lux and with the Lisbon girls as a group. The boys' space is set as the neighborhood boys hanging out together, either on the street or at one of the homes. All of these spaces include characteristic music to connect with the characters and the dramatic situation.

The first two spaces—the family space and the shared teen space—are branded with songs from soft rock. These spaces offer music that would appeal to the 1970s teen, but would also be 'acceptable' to their parents. The family space is the downstairs rec room in the Lisbon home. In this space, the Lisbon family hosts the party for Cecilia and her sisters hoping to socialize the girls in a more meaningful way. Consequently, we must assume that the music selected for the party has been approved by the parents, probably from among choices in their daughters' record collection. Alternately, the girls might have chosen the songs knowing that any selection would have to be palatable to their parents. Todd Rundgren's 'A Dream Goes on Forever' and the Hollies' 'The Air That I Breathe' are the records played during the party. On the surface, both are innocuous, simple rock ballads, bordering on MOR music. Closer examination reveals songs that reflect directly on the main themes of the film. 'A Dream Goes on Forever' conjures images of a dream that spans across time and space driven by love and obsession. While the song suggests romantic longing, it is one that remains unrequited and unfulfilled. As the song concludes: 'You're so far away and so long ago/But my dream goes on forever/And how much I loved you you'll never know/Till you join me within my dream.' The stanza fits perfectly with the romantic obsession of the middle-aged men from the neighborhood. Their dream of the Lisbon sisters goes on, but memory, time and death all make sure that their dream will always slip away. 'The Air That I Breathe' similarly presents a case of obsession. 'Sometimes all I need is the air that I breathe/And to love you' proclaims the 1974 hit by the British pop/rock group The Hollies. The opening chorus of the song which recounts a man foregoing all comforts in life just to be with his lover. Again, obsession and a clear (maniacal?) focus on the beloved. Suddenly, two songs which appear to be so bland actually comment on the dark themes of the film, albeit in a soft rock way that the whole Lisbon family can appreciate.

The locus for shared teen space music is the dance in which Trip and Lux are crowned Homecoming King and Queen. Unlike the family space music with the undertone of dark obsession, the music in the teen shared space focuses primarily on a lighter male/female dynamic of mutual attraction: the mystical 'Strange Magic' by ELO, the soft ballad 'I'm Not in Love' by 10cc, and the rock anthem 'Come Sail Away' by Styx. From the dreamy 'I'm Not in Love' to the energy of both 'Strange Magic' and 'Come Sail Away,' the songs in the shared teen space offer an affirmation of the journey for attraction and love. Unencumbered by the adult influence, the songs are more contemporary and edgy than the selections in the family space. The teen space songs present a promising view of sexual attraction and romantic coupling. The energy and life force of youth are preserved in these songs. Coppola uses them to present a healthy and dynamic picture of adolescence and sexuality.

The musical choices become much starker in those branded as primarily female or male. Coppola purposefully uses two songs by Heart, the mid-1970s rock group known best for its members, sisters Ann and Nancy Wilson. The Wilson sisters were among the very first female rockers, although Heart was a mixed gender band. The iconic image of the sisters on the 1976 cover of their first record album, *Dreamboat Annie*, features them back-to-back, defiantly posed against a red heart set between them. The Wilsons, secure in their musical and sexual power, commented, 'We don't try to be like men and we don't go in for heavy feminine bit either' (Carson et al. 2015: 88–89). Coppola links the Wilson sisters and the Lisbon sisters, but the connection is made most directly with Lux. Like Ann and Nancy Wilson, Lux is an independent force whose sexuality and power cannot be easily accommodated by the mainstream.

Heart's hit 'Magic Man' introduces the viewers to Trip Fontaine. As the camera pans up his body, the narrator explains, 'But the only reliable boy who actually got to know Lux was Trip Fontaine who, only eight months before the suicides, had emerged from baby fat to the delight of girls and mothers alike.' After a brief scene of Trip flirting with a school clerk to receive a dismissal slip, Coppola cuts to Trip entering the high school. This scene of

Trip walking freezes the film—it becomes a music video rather than merely introducing a supporting character. Against Heart attesting to the powers of the 'magic man,' Trip removes his sunglasses and saunters through the hallway, leather jacket slung confidently over his shoulder (see Figure 4.1). All the schoolgirls react in an exaggerated way to Trip: swooning, giggling and blatantly surveying Trip's body. The song continues against shots of Trip entering classrooms, lounging in his pool, greeting a girl at his door, and smoking pot in his car before class. The video ends with Heart meanwhile pleading, 'You don't have to love me yet/Let's get high awhile/But try to understand/Try to understand/Try, try, try to understand/I'm a magic man.' The lyrics match the character perfectly, even to Trip's chronic habit of smoking pot. Rather than sketch the character initially through dialog and interaction, Coppola uses this music video pastiche to define Trip Fontaine. With the female vocal from Heart, the alignment between lyric and character, and the clear objectification of the male body, the Trip 'Magic Man' video shows how Coppola can adroitly use music and music video conventions as a potent form of storytelling.

The connection between Lux, Trip and music is continued with Coppola's other treatment of a Heart song, 'Crazy on You.' After Trip visits the Lisbon home to watch television with the family, he waits outside in his sports car for a few minutes. With the instrumental of Heart's song accompanying the close shot of Trip behind the wheel, suddenly Lux bursts into

Figure 4.1 Trip Fontaine, the 'Magic Man' of *The Virgin Suicides*

the car. Wearing just her nightdress, Lux devours Trip, passionately kissing, fondling and embracing him. It is, by far, the most sexual moment in the film, driven entirely by Lux and her attraction for Trip. Heart's song, meanwhile, reaches its refrain: 'And my love, the pleasure's mine/Let me go crazy on you.' As with 'Magic Man,' Coppola uses this song directly and strategically. The lyrics and the hard rock rhythm stand in for Lux and her feelings. The viewer understands more about the character and her motivation than would be possible through conventional dramatic exposition.

Coppola saves the other musical set piece for late in the film. The sisters have been forbidden to leave the house, and, after months of this shutdown, the boys are desperate to connect with the girls. Keep in mind, however, that we do not see any relaxed or natural communication between the Lisbon sisters and the neighborhood boys earlier in the film. The most extensive interaction comes at the rec room party which is abruptly ended by Cecilia's suicide. After this point, the boys try to connect with the girls, with little success. After the school year has started, at the lockers, Chase introduces himself to Mary. She responds blankly, 'I know who you are. I've only been going to this school my whole life. You don't have to talk to me.' The fascination of the boys only increases though. They sift through Cecilia's diary and imagine incidents involving Cecilia and her sisters. When the home shutdown occurs, the boys first start to 'interact' with the girls through ordering the same travel catalogs and imagining shared trips. The boys decide to call the Lisbon sisters. Rather than risk rejection, instead of talking, the boys merely play a song and hold the phone receiver to the record player. Tim Anderson suggests that playing records comments on the past, and can hinder a character's ability to communicate in the present (2008: 51–76). In this way, the boys chose to substitute their music choices for conversation.

This choice may not seem as curious as it first appears. Adolescent therapy has often relied on the use of music as a means to connect with teens. In some settings, music is used to illuminate the inner world of the teen as a means to express what they cannot verbally. Adolescents are encouraged to bring their choice of music to the therapy session. Eventually the therapist works on having the teen explain their music and why the music was crucial to them. In this way, music therapy with adolescents improves the understanding of teens' motivations and their relationship with others. The emphasis in therapy is on how music can be linked to identity formation and the development of social skills (McFerran 2010: 41). As Katrina McFerran describes the process, 'The focus on identity formation and social skill is a positive outcome of this traditional orientation to music therapy with teenagers. "Who am I?" is an important question to be addressed throughout life, but it gains prominence during this phase of peak intellectual and physical capacity' (45). While not speaking specifically of the adolescent experience, Jacques Attali reminds us that music is a power for socializing overall:

To my way of thinking, music appears in myth as an affirmation that society is possible. That is the essential thing. Its order simulates the social order, and its dissonances express marginalities. The code of music simulates the accepted rules of society.

(1985: 29)

Through the musical 'game' imposed by the boys, the Lisbon sisters are actually given a means for self-expression to increase their socialization. The game can help to restore the social order that has been broken by their parents' harsh punishments and enforced social exile. The Lisbon sisters are able to bolster self-awareness and confidence through their musical selections and through their response to the boys' musical choices.

This self-expression through the musical choices is even more significant since music can provide the marginalized an idealized form of how life could be. Simon Frith posits that this is, indeed, a crucial aspect of music's power, making it carry a political valence (1984: 59–69). The oppositional power of music is set, once again, against space. As Lesley Pruitt suggests, young males are expected to engage with music in the streets, while young women enjoy music in private spaces, such as their bedrooms (2013: 121). Pruitt's project looks at a specific use of music as a means to transform conflict and to 'build peace.' She concludes that often the creation of a 'third space' is crucial for these efforts at peace building (127). Interestingly, the concept of the third space is helpful to understand the music playing in *The Virgin Suicides*. The girls' space is now almost a prison: they are housebound and spend all their time together in one of the larger bedrooms. The boys' space includes various bedrooms from the neighborhood boys. Each group is constrained by their space and by their failure to communicate. Using the records through the phone calls opens up a new space. This space is a neutral one that is shared between the boys and the girls. The space is defined entirely by the record choices by the girls and boys. Apart from a few cursory words, no other communication is offered by either group.

The structure of this record communication, by design, places a great significance on which records are chosen by the groups. Each record is a chance to express feelings and make a link to others. Robyn J. Stilwell notes an important aspect to the girls' choices. With Mrs. Lisbon either burning or disposing of Lux's rock records, the girls are left with the more innocuous singer-songwriters (2006: 152–166). The first record—'Hello, It's Me'— is played by the boys with a curt 'call us' before they hang up after the song ends. Apart from the obvious salutation, the song by Todd Rundgren also connects to the earlier rec room party scene which used Rundgren's 'A Dream Goes on Forever.' Like that first song, 'Hello, It's Me,' presents someone pining after an unrequited love. Certainly, the song works as a way for the boys to express their desire for connection. It also obliquely gestures to the confinement ('It's important to me/That you know you are free/'Cause I never want to make you change for me') of the girls and to the boys' desire to offer support and companionship. A later song for the boys, the Bee Gees' 'Run to Me,' pushes the connection even further. Rather than offer a neutral greeting, the boys' second song issues a call-to-action: 'Run to me whenever you're lonely (to love me)/Run to me if you need a shoulder.' The boys' choice of songs creates a simple narrative, ending with the girls seeking refuge through the boys.

The girls' song choices are more alarming, but just as revealing of their motivation as the boys' ones. In response to 'Hello, It's Me,' the girls return by playing 'Alone Again (Naturally).' The ballad was a huge hit in 1972 for Irish singer Gilbert O'Sullivan, spending six weeks as #1 on Billboard Magazine's Hot 100 Singles Chart. The ballad tells of a man desperate after being left at the altar by his fiancée. After this anecdote, the song's narrator tells of his father's death and his suicidal ideation. The narrator is now, and will be in the future, simply alone again, naturally. To place the song in context, certainly the mid-1970s were a time when issues of mental illness and suicidal ideation were not understood or addressed to the extent they are currently. Still, even if the song is treated as just an indication of mood and atmosphere, the message is clearly stated: you cannot rely on others, and all routes lead sooner or later to the grave.

The boys' response to 'Alone Again (Naturally)' is the Bee Gees' 'Run to Me.' The girls return this call with Carole King's 'So Far Away.' The song is a wistful ballad mourning being apart from a special person, longing for connection but knowing that it cannot happen. In the context of Carole King's work, Sheila Weller believes that the song is one of three that 'puzzle out a new idea of "home"' (2008: 323). The song suggests that we are ruled by impermanence ('Doesn't anybody stay in one place anymore?'). Clearly, there is a longing for home, but no solutions or opportunities are presented. The parallels of the song to the Lisbon girls' situation are persuasive: despite being locked at home, the girls have lost all of the positive aspects (warmth, comfort, support) that are usually associated with home. They are emotionally adrift like King's narrator. The Lisbon girls similarly have no idea if 'home' is even possible anymore given their circumstances. King denounces impermanence, yet fails to suggest any solutions or hope. Do the Lisbon sisters feel that there are no solutions, that 'home' has been lost? Further, if the song is viewed as a response to the boys playing 'Run to Me,' the Lisbon sisters appear to be saying that any kind of union is impossible. They cannot run to the boys, leaving them forever 'so far away.'

Analyzing the conclusion through the framework of these songs helps to explain the devastating mass suicide. If the boys had paid attention to the specifics of the girls' song choices, they would be alerted to the suicidal ideation, the depression, and the apparent lack of options open to the girls. The boys' songs are pushing for the girls to join them, in romance and friendship. Rather than comprehend the message given by the girls, the boys imagine an escape ride for all of them gliding down the highway, with sunshine, open windows, and laughter. The boys have committed to their fantasy of uniting with the girls, disregarding the signs offered to them. Despite the opportunity of a 'third space' for building relationships, ultimately the records are yet another failure of communication. The boys' conclusion is that the girls want an escape trip. They show up at the Lisbon home with an elaborate plan to liberate the girls and to go on a vacation together. The plan is entirely from the perspective of the boys. The girls, in fact, are asking the boys to be witnesses to their termination of life. Music in *The Virgin Suicides* allows for self-expression, but it cannot build a bridge between the girls and the boys.

Through the original score by Air and the use of classic songs from the 1970s, Coppola demonstrates how effective music can be as a storytelling device. Music is used as a key structuring force, internally within the film and externally through the soundtrack albums. With the Air score, the film creates a strong exchange with synthesized music of the 1970s, along with a sense of cultural dislocation. With the popular songs, the film explains different spaces and their function, in addition to allowing the characters to speak through the music. Eugenides' novel is faithfully adapted, but the points where the viewer can really appreciate Coppola's artistry is through the visual and aural components of the storytelling. The music is placed in a dialog with the other textual elements. Viewers can experience a richer and more textured cinematic world due to the ways that Coppola allows the score and song choices to work with, and at times against, the text. In this way, Coppola gives context to the decisions and actions of her characters. While music may seem like mere incidental accompaniment, the film illustrates how music can be a driving force to create the world of the film and to offer commentary on the characters and their dramatic situations.

Notes

1. Even though Air composed the soundtrack for *The Virgin Suicides*, Coppola used an instrumental track from Fatboy Slim's 'Right Here, Right Now' in the film's trailer. Her allegiance appears to be strong to this brand of electronic and ambient music.
2. For an interesting overview of the progression of the French Electronic music scene and the use of vocals as part of the music, consult Smith (2004).

5   The Advertising Aesthetic and Youth Culture of *The Virgin Suicides*

The Virgin Suicides is a film deeply implicated in the world of advertising. Coppola certainly has an appreciation for film history, but her film illustrates that she understands, in a profound way, the impact of advertising, marketing and mass media representations. The film's most distinctive visual flourishes are linked to the tropes of advertising. Coppola is channeling key images in the film from an array of cosmetics, fashion and health ads from the 1970s. This connection is made both explicitly and implicitly within the film: the neighborhood boys are inspired by advertising and actively create imaginative shots and scenes that feel heavily indebted to the images and icons of 1970s advertising. Through identifying and tracing the usage of these advertising-like images, Coppola's distinctive visual style becomes apparent. This visual style starts with *The Virgin Suicides* and continues not just through the subsequent films, but also pointedly through several later commercials directed by Coppola. The visual style of *The Virgin Suicides* deepens and resonates through these commercials. This road leads eventually to the striking commercials for the perfume Daisy by Marc Jacobs in 2013. These commercial images of a group of teen girls luxuriating on a summer's day could easily be the Lisbon sisters, transported away from the suburban home by their fantasies and the promise of a better life through advertising.

Visual Bursts and Style

Although much of *The Virgin Suicides* plays out as a straight melodrama with conventional shooting and editing choices, certain key visual elements in the film are highlighted by Coppola. These moments break the diegetic world, creating a space for joy and happiness for the characters. Dreamlike in design, these reveries represent a high water mark for the characters: their dreams and fantasies become real through these bursts of visual energy. The first sustained instance of this visual style occurs with student Peter Sisten using the bathroom after dinner at the Lisbon home. Sisten, obsessed by the girls who have been flirting with him, walks through Cecilia's bedroom to reach the upstairs bathroom. He smells the girls' perfume, opens the bathroom cupboard to find boxes of tampons, and raises a lipstick to smell its fragrance. At that moment, the music swells and the screen fills with a backlit Lux tossing her hair and closing her eyes seductively. The reverie is broken by Lux tapping on the door. Peter Sisten's imagination of Lux is tied deliberately by Coppola to the exploration of products in the bathroom. Through accessing the product, he conjures the image of a seductive Lux (see Figures 5.1a and 5.1b). The image however is impersonal, devoid of a

(a)

(b)

Figure 5.1a and 5.1b Lux adrift in advertising imagery?

personal connection to Peter. It is just an imagination inspired as much by the product advertising as by Lux's flirtations at dinner. This bold appearance by Lux, apparently existing in the imagination rather than the real world is repeated at several times in the film. Coppola uses close shots of Lux directly addressing the camera (e.g., winking at the camera before the titles), isolating intimate moments of Lux (e.g., brushing the grass off her shoulder while flirting with the boy) and even in enhanced moments of real action. The latter would include the shot of Lux turning to Trip on meeting him for the first time. Coppola offers a little CGI glint from Lux's eye: her eyes literally sparkle at Trip.

The other visual bursts are connected to specific stimuli within the film: Cecilia's diary, the travel catalogs, and the final imaginary road trip taken by the sisters and the neighborhood boys. As with the Lux appearances, these visual stylistics evoke a joyful, exuberant mood. These visuals present moments of bliss from the perspective of the neighborhood boys. Each of these is either directly or indirectly linked to advertising of the period. This connection makes sense though as well. For the teen boys, the world of mass media is the place most often associated with pleasure, fantasy and wish fulfillment. Their dreams borrow from the styles and treatments illustrated in the commercials and advertising.

There are differences worth noting in the manifestations of these visual bursts by the neighborhood boys. In the first sequence, the boys are reviewing Cecilia's diary, supposedly obtained by nefarious means from the plumber's son. The images appear to be from the perspective of one of the boys although it is unclear whether we are seeing the narrator's vision or the boy who is reading from the diary at that moment. Certain scenes are dramatized directly from the diary text, such as Lux stroking the whale. Others, however, are unanchored: Cecilia writing in her diary sitting in a golden field, a close-up of Lux's eye, and the sisters playing on a swing. Still other images connect with words in the diary, although they are not narrated directly by the boys: a unicorn, blowing on a dandelion, and hula dancing by the sisters. The sequence starts with a direct dramatization from the diary, but ends in a torrent of unrelated images testifying to the beauty, joy and mystery of the Lisbon sisters. The viewer is left with a sister playing with a sparkler, blowing on a dandelion and hula dancing. Images once static are sometimes combined: Lux jumping up and down in split screen with the unicorn; Cecilia writing in the field superimposed on a close shot of Lux's eye and her hair gently moving in the wind; Mary blows on the dandelion while Lux stares on, in an obvious split screen composition. The specific reference to the diary dissolves into an array of images connoting fun and abandonment.

The fleeting images of the girls, especially Lux, could easily be part of an ad campaign. The mood is light, fun and energetic, which could match with any number of ads targeting teens and young adults. Returning to the era of *The Virgin Suicides*, the mid-1970s, print advertising evokes many of the same visual and emotional appeals as the clips from the film. The period foregrounded the 'blonde next door' from Cybill Shepherd (who started in modeling) and Farrah Fawcett Majors, linking directly to the blonde goddesses of Coppola's film. Visual touches from *The Virgin Suicides* appear to be inspired, directly or indirectly, from the ads of the era: the golden-hued background, figures sitting adrift in a field, extreme close-ups of faces, and, of course, the bold yellows characteristic of the decade (see Figures 5.2a–5.2d). With the visual bursts, Coppola isolates specific images and

(a)

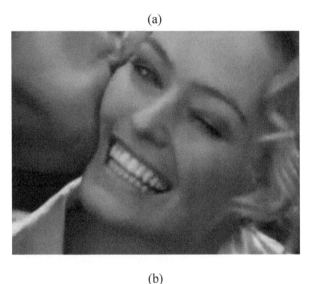

(b)

Figure 5.2a to 5.2d Golden visions in 1970s advertising

(c)

(d)

Figure 5.2a to 5.2d (Continued)

moments filtering them through typical advertising icons from the era. The style is fragmentary, but also evocative. Just as advertising promises a better life and world through consumption of the product, so does Coppola with the visual bursts. Keep in mind that these are motivated by the neighborhood boys, and connected to products, worlds or figments of their imaginations. The boys' fantasy of the Lisbon girls gets coded into the mini-narratives of advertising and commercial culture. Through these reference points, the boys are able to contain and control their passion for Lux and the other sisters.

Visual bursts are also present in the sequence about the shared travel cata-logs. Locked away in their home, the Lisbon sisters order travel catalogs to imagine escapes around the globe. Noticing the catalogs in the daily mail, the neighborhood boys also obtain the same catalogs as a way to bond with the girls. As the narrator recounts, the catalogs inspired 'impossible excur-sions that have scarred us forever, making us happier with dreams than our lives.' As the boys peruse the ads for international tours and adventures, the viewer sees imagined snapshots of the boys and the Lisbon girls on these vacations. The static pictures offer a variety of silly poses, grins and smirks. In all, the boys are embracing one or more of the Lisbon sisters. Occasion-ally, a shot includes only a boy/girl couple; most are focused on the group having fun in the vacation locale. In this exercise, 'even Cecilia is saved' as the boys imagine her as a bride in India, praying while wearing a full sari. The boys take the advertising photos and copy and imagine a series of 'impossible excursions' as a means to get closer to the sisters.

These advertising inspired photos connect with a powerful scene from the film's conclusion. As the boys wait in the Lisbon home, they imagine their fantasy road trip with the sisters. In the cavernous 1970s station wagon, the teens drive along the freeway on a beautiful sunny afternoon. The windows are open, with the sisters and boys sitting closely and comfortably with each other. The escape is possible.

Almost all of these moments are associated with joy and enthusiasm, soaked in the sun and sustaining for years to come. Visually, Coppola also integrates the occasional static compositions, such as Cecilia sinking into her bathtub after her first suicide attempt or Lux waking up, in a close shot, against the blue skies of the stadium (see Figures 5.3a and 5.3b). Unlike the other visual bursts, these ones are emotional, but in a negative sense. They are associated with a melancholy and sadness that infuses so much of the film.

Unlike the upbeat images, these melancholic ones have either slow movement or none at all. Coppola is interested in a quiet contemplation of the image rather than creating a positive mood or environment. The precise composition and use of color suggest a print ad for an unknown product. Youth, beauty and aesthetics combine to create these quiet images just as powerful as the sunswept ones.

In the Context of 1970s Advertising

The blurring of the diegetic world with the world of advertising is moti-vated, first and foremost, by the teenage protagonists. Teenagers have a complicated relationship with advertising. As Deborah Roeder John sug-gests, teens are aware of the multiple perspectives contained in ads, but they

Figure 5.3a and 5.3b Lux wakes up in a blue haze suggesting a static advertising image

nevertheless use ads as a crucial means to shape their own identity and to conform to group expectations. John describes teens as being in a 'reflective stage' in their consumption of advertising. This does not necessarily translate into teens being more discerning in their responses to advertising or to the inherent manipulation that may occurs in ads (1999: 187). In fact, teens may be more susceptible to advertising since they are searching to create their own identities through appropriating icons and elements shown in ads.

The 1970s, the decade of *The Virgin Suicides*, also evidenced a firestorm of activity around the issues of youth and advertising. In 1970, Peggy Charren founded Action for Children's Television (ACT), a lobbying group inspired by the overcommercialization and poor quality of children's television. ACT was instrumental in fighting for FCC guidelines covering advertising and children's television (Montgomery 1989: 14–15). In 1973, ACT was successful in lobbying the National Association for Broadcasters to limit commercials to 12 minutes per hour and to prohibit hosts for children's television from appearing in commercials. A key tenet of ACT was the need to protect children from excessive and manipulative advertising (Cross 2002: 441–447). ACT realized that this task was hampered by the parents' need to express love through buying products and gifts for their children. In this way, their efforts needed to be targeted as much to parents as to children.

Despite these efforts, the decade also evidenced a continual tension between advertising and sexuality. Most conspicuously the Calvin Klein jean ads with teenager Brooke Shields crystallized the terms of the debate. A series of seven commercials, the Calvin Klein spots offered 15-year-old Shields in a variety of situations alluding to intimacy and sexuality. In the most famous ad ('Feminist'), the single line of dialog in the 30 second commercial was deliberately ambiguous and sexual: 'You want to know what comes between me and my Calvins? Nothing.' Given that Shields had played a prostitute's child who auctioned her virginity to the highest bidder in Louis Malle's *Pretty Baby* (1978), the media was prepared to see Shields as the young object of adult desire. With Shields' provocative poses and seductive line readings, the ads highlighted a major issue of the era: using children or young teens as a focus for adult sexual interest. Although the overt content of the ads was not pornographic, the suggestiveness was blatant, making some uncomfortable and upset (Simpson 1981: 390–400).

These controversies are mapped against two divergent tendencies. As Thomas Hine describes in his review of 1970s culture, *The Great Funk* (2007) the decade was informed by a high level of both tolerance and acceptance (22). Working through the impact of the social movements from the 1960s, a range of behaviors were not just tolerated but encouraged. Ads appeared that were both openly sexual in nature and adhering to a very limited view of girls and women. The concern centered on the very limited number of roles open to women in advertising images, especially the attractive younger adult and the housewife/mother (Schneider and Barich Schneider 1979: 79–84). Focusing on the negative imagery, Jean Kilbourne, creator of the 'Killing Us Softly: Advertising's Image of Women' film series, makes a strong argument for the regressive power of 1970s advertising:

[Ads in the 1970s] were very blatantly sexist. In those days, there was no consciousness about the fact that this might not be a good idea or that this might be offensive. So [advertisers] were able to get away with an ad for a feminine hygiene spray that said, 'Feminine odor is everyone's problem.' Or a cigarette ad where a woman said, 'My boyfriend told me he loved me for my mind. I was never so insulted in my life.'
(quoted in Angley 2015)

At the same time, limits on this way of thinking were evident in many quarters (Hine 2007: 22 and 75). Feminist consciousness-raising sought to inform women of the dangers posed by patriarchal society. Understanding how the media helped to create stereotypical and sexist images and roles for women became a key part of the feminist agenda. To craft images that were not patriarchal or supporting traditional roles and placement was therefore a central goal of much feminist media analysis of the time. Judith Williamson's classic 1978 text, *Decoding Advertisements: Ideology and Meaning in Advertising*, traces the process through which advertising transparently contains ideas and functions to support the dominant ideology and economic base of society. As Williamson notes, we need to alter our perceptions of this covert form of propaganda to expand roles for all those who fall outside the dominant patriarchal system (1978: 13).

The tensions between regressive and more progressive forces are evident in the print ads of the period. The predominant message of the time was clear; as Megan Garber explains it, 'And what women of the '70s really wanted, the (mostly male, mostly white) advertisers of the time assumed, was similar to what many of them still want today, despite all the progress that has been made in the meantime: to be attractive to men' (2015). Speaking directly to that tendency, Love's Baby Soft Cosmetics dresses a lollypop sucking young woman like a little girl set against the tagline 'Because Innocence is Sexier than You Think' (see Figure 5.4). The ad underlines the female teen sexuality and the line between innocence and experience (played ironically since the adult is dressed as a child). The image is in line with the Brooke Shields Calvin Klein ads, as is the suggestion that sexualizing childhood is to be encouraged. Other ads may not be so overtly sexual and may appear, at first glance, to be empowering.

Figure 5.4 Sexualizing the prepubescent girl, Love's Baby Soft, 1975

Nevertheless, these ads argue that young women can only be attractive by consuming their product. Cover Girl Clean Make Up, for instance, stresses 'fresh, clean, clear' which apparently can be achieved as a look through using their products. Carnation's Instant Breakfast claims 'A Body Couldn't Ask for Anything More' next to a shot of a young woman in overalls and workman's cap ('girls take charge!'), but showing her long legs and curves at the same time. Young 'N Free deodorant features the sketch of a female teen, in flowered pants and long flowing blonde hair, with the line 'Learn to be Pretty with Young 'N Free.' In the 1970s, the message was clear: to either be the object of sexual desire or to create yourself to be as desirable as possible. Product consumption was important to this path for the young people. As Thomas Frank describes it, 'Liberation is a matter of consuming' (1997: 156).

Tellingly, these concerns have persisted over the decades. Looking at the landscape for provocative advertising, content analysis of ads between 1964 and 1984 illustrated that the level of sexual content in ads did not shift discernably. There was, however, a marked increase in sexual content of ads in general interest magazines. This tended to be visual rather than verbal in design. In particular, the male/female contact in the ads tripled during this period (Soley and Kurzbard 1986: 45–54 and 54). In 2006, the American Psychological Association (APA) convened a Task Force to study the impact of presenting sexual images in the media and advertisements. Reporting in 2012, the Task Force concluded that magazine advertisements more frequently sexually objectified women than men. In fact, women were three times more likely to be dressed in a sexually provocative style com-pared to men in these ads. Echoing past findings, the study also demon-strated that girls and women were far more likely to be objectified than boys and men. Further, the APA Task Force found that girls applied models of behavior and image from the advertising and the mass media as formative in their behaviors, self-concepts, and identities. In this way, the power of advertising to create images for the girls was seen as one of the most crucial impacts of the mass media (McCall 2012).

Advertising Ideology, Fantasy & Narrative

The impact of this advertising discourse on the young has largely been viewed as consequential. In varying degrees, the advertising imagery serves to create a world with set roles, ideology and functioning. Gary Cross describes this fabricated world as a fantasy culture: 'The images, goods and rituals of a commercialized childhood led to a fantasy culture from which parents were excluded and which appeared to be anything but innocent' (2002: 445). In this world, the teen is able to pursue ideas, needs and dreams based on their mass mediated commercial world rather than their immediate one. On the positive side, this commercialized world can help youth navigate a period of dramatic transition and change in their lives.

What are the consequences though of using this fantasy world as a means to navigate adolescent change? As Williamson would attest, the ideological implications of the ad world are far-reaching. The open avenues for romance, sexual expression, and freedom of expression were much more evident by the mid-1970s. The neighborhood boys in *The Virgin Suicides* are part of a 'fantasy world' defined by records, mass culture, advertising and consumer products. Their experiences are informed by, among other aspects, the advertising culture pinpointed so aptly by Williamson. The advertising culture is shaped by an ideology with traditional gender roles and by the all-encompassing need for girls to be attractive at any cost.

In *The Virgin Suicides*, this ideology of advertising is illustrated in several different ways. At the start, the narrator talks of the boys, now men, trying 'to put the pieces together' in the Lisbon story. The visual advertising bursts are obvious 'pieces.' They are derived from advertising images and tropes. Even more pervasive is the film's insistence on the myriad occasions in which Coppola structures the moments of voyeurism. Following the central tenets of advertising of that time, young women are constructed to maximize their 'to-be-looked-at'-ness. In this way, there are multiple occasions within the story centered on male voyeurism of the girls. Usually the object of desire is Lux, but there are certainly other examples in the film. Consider Dominic's obsession with Diana Porter (he jumps out of the window falling onto the garden hedge to signify his love). Coppola carefully shoots the scene with Dominic watching Diana play tennis. The tennis game plays out in slow motion, emphasizing the movement of Diana's body. Coppola even cuts to an extreme close shot of Diana wiping the sweat off her brow. The shot is remarkable for focusing on such a very specific detail, for showing the level of detail and fascination offered by the female figure for this boy.

Due to the divide between the boys and girls, their 'relationship' takes on a largely visual component. The neighborhood boy/s stare at Lux (sitting outside their math class, making out with a boy on the roof, having lunch with her sisters outside), building her into this object of fantasy. So many of these voyeuristic scenes are presented with Lux as the focus of attention. Despite professing interest in the 'beautiful creatures' otherwise known as the Lisbon sisters, ultimately the boys choose to concentrate on the under-age Lux. Lux's aggressive sexuality and open display of sexual interest fit with the advertising fantasy of the sexually free young girl. The other sisters, attractive but more in line with the middle-class Catholic world of the parents, fail to fuel their fantasies in the same way. As a result, much of the objectification is centered on Lux, including the coy 'see-through' shots of her underwear with the boy's name written on it. If advertising places such emphasis on the attractive female and the male's role as aggressor, can we be surprised that the fantasy of Lux Lisbon in the film culminates with Trip Fontaine seducing Lux and leaving her on the football field after his conquest? Lux's sexuality and precociousness make her the ideal target for the advertising fantasy, whether as a visual imagination of Lux hula dancing or as a narrative climax of Lux being seduced and abandoned.

Advertising is based on a call-to-action, to make the consumer purchase a product or service. Apart from the sexual dynamics at play in the film, so much of the world in *The Virgin Suicides* is placed specifically in this commercial world. Coppola is very precise in including artifacts, products and icons of 1970s consumer culture to build the Lisbon household. Much attention is placed not just on the dialog and interactions between the characters but on the mise-en-scène constructed so carefully with 1970s consumer culture. Coppola treats the Lisbon home as another character in the film. Notice how carefully the rooms are detailed, especially Cecilia's room (see Figure 5.5) and the 'shared' room by the sisters after the lockdown. As a neighbor comments on Cecilia's suicide attempt, 'She wanted out of that decorating scheme!' The Lisbon home, with amassing clutter and little upscale taste, is marked as suspect by this neighbor.

The film is distinguished by an evocative and detailed production design. Viewers are invited to become part of this world. Consider the simple scene of visitor Peter Sisten using the bathroom by Cecilia's room. The film purposefully illustrates his route through the home to reach this space. He

Figure 5.5 The detailed mise-en-scène, Cecilia's bedroom

pauses to notice all the stickers on Cecilia's door, the religious icons, doll tea service, tarot card, and toys on her floor, and the world created through this mass of objects cluttered through the room. This world in the Lisbon household includes the religious iconography cards, the instamatic camera, the decorative bracelets, and the 1970s teen fashions on display so prominently. As Jeanne R. Steele and Jane D. Brown explain, the adolescent room is a crucial space for understanding their identity. In this space, the teens engage with mass media as a means to construct their developing identities and to create a sense of individuation (1995: 551–576). After the mass suicide and the departure of the Lisbon parents, Coppola closes with a tour of the emptied house. Now all that is left are the commercial artifacts, tagged with prices for a yard sale. What remains at the end are just the detritus of consumer culture, with little or no value. Even Lux's homecoming queen tiara is tagged for a quick sale. Coppola saves this final melancholy review of the consumer goods as a marker for her lost characters. Ultimately, the remnants of consumerism are all that remains of the Lisbon family. These are the 'pieces' of the puzzle that can be retrieved by the neighborhood boys.

Sofia Coppola's Commercial Aesthetic

The links between the style of *The Virgin Suicides* and advertising are many. The visual bursts and static compositions echo advertising design. The attention to detail and layered mise-en-scène recall a concentrated environment or world often associated with advertising and marketing. Music is used both nostalgically and as a means to evoke a strong sense of emotion. These traits are not just emblematic of *The Virgin Suicides*, they also help to create a road map for Coppola's parallel career in commercial advertising. In between film shoots, Coppola has been incredibly active with a parallel career directing television commercials. Since 2008, Coppola has directed, among others, spots for Miss Dior Cherie, Marni for H&M, Daisy perfume by Marc Jacobs, The Gap, Calvin Klein underwear, and Panthére jewelry watch for Cartier. Coppola's ability to characterize a mood, story, and, to a much lesser extent, a product in either 30 or 60 seconds is remarkable. She is able to create these commercials through the same sense of visual bursts, matched with occasional static compositions, defining the commercial aesthetic of *The Virgin Suicides*. Coppola encapsulates an entire world in the space of either 30 or 60 seconds, and the economy with which she is able to accomplish this is impressive. Those who criticize Coppola for being dependent on environment rather than plot in her features need to review her commercials.[1] In these, it is clear that creating space is the narrative; the director succinctly and accurately captures an environment and mood that suggest a potential range of actions.

Three examples illustrate the ways that Coppola has translated her commercial visual style in *The Virgin Suicides* directly to television commercials.

With rare exceptions, her commercials follow the visual bursts in Coppola's first film.[2] They serve a similar thematic purpose as well: the spots are designed to isolate moments of happiness and joy within a very specific and detailed mise-en-scène. Music is used strategically to evoke a past time. The sum of the shots is far greater than the individual images in these spots. Within 60 seconds, Coppola is able to create a mini-world and to invite the viewer to take part in it. Conspicuous (product) consumption is a by-product of the commercial rather than being central. In this way, Coppola's commercials could be seen as directorial exercises. They develop her distinctive visual and aural styles, and let her create, under the duress of a single minute or less, a completely realized mood and world.

For the 2012 one-minute spot for the clothing brand Marni for H&M, Coppola transports the fantasy road trip from *Suicides* to the town of Marrakesh. The commercial features a shot of a road trip with open car windows, blowing hair and beautiful sunlight. In the Marni commercial, Coppola achieves two goals: to create a sustained mood and to suggest a narrative. The spot has no dialog. It is replaced by Roxy Music's elegiac 'Avalon,' featuring vocals by Bryan Ferry. Coppola cast British actress Imogen Poots in the lead role since she reminded her of Marisa Berenson, 'able to convey so much without speaking or doing very much.'[3] Imogen lounges by the pool, waking from a reverie. She spots a handsome young man across the yard. Ferry proclaims, 'Now the party's over, I'm so tired . . .' Brief shots of the partying (last night?) ensue with beautiful young women and men chatting, flirting and watching each other in the opulent Moroccan setting. Imogen has a chaste kiss in the pool with the handsome young man. Just as she captured mid-1970s Michigan so perfectly, Coppola is able to sketch most clearly a group of striking, presumably rich young people relaxing and effortlessly finding love in the Moroccan desert. The fashion prints of Marni blend against the brownish, baroque Moroccan architecture and the palm trees. At the end of the spot, Coppola returns to Imogen waking on the chaise, albeit in a different outfit (see Figure 5.6a). Did Imogen simply dream the party and romance? This ambiguity gives the spot a slightly melancholic feel. Within the moments of happiness and abandonment, there is always the possibility of absence and loss.

In 2013, Coppola directed a 30-second Daisy perfume spot for Marc Jacobs. Jacobs is a long-time Coppola friend and designer who refers to Coppola as his muse (Blasberg 2014). Unlike the Marni spot, the Daisy commercial fits directly into *The Virgin Suicides* world. The petals of a daisy are removed one by one. Several beautiful young ladies cavort in a field of daisies, wearing long, white robes and dresses. The effect is an ersatz hippie vibe settled into a sun-drenched daisy field. One of the girls makes a daisy chain and is seen later wearing a crown of daisies. The second location is a riverside. The same group of girls chat, read and relax. A hammock offers a nice refuge, but the scene is

Figure 5.6a to 5.6c Marni for H&M, Daisy by Marc Jacobs, Panthére by Cartier: Coppola commercials channeling the visual bursts of *The Virgin Suicides*

(c)

Figure 5.6a to 5.6c (Continued)

one of deep bonding and quiet enjoyment of nature's beauty and, of course, each other. The spot ends with the bottles of Daisy perfume, three placed side-by-side. There is racial and ethnic diversity among the girls, but otherwise the Lisbon sisters could easily play these roles. The specific visual link to *The Virgin Suicides* is Cecilia writing in her diary in the field of flowers. Tonally though, the girl-bonding, light fun, and supremely sunny moments in the commercial feel like they could simply be out-takes from *The Virgin Suicides* (see Figure 5.6b). The reveries from the film have been revived for a new group of girls, perfectly comfortable with their company and secret to the world.

By 2017, Coppola infused her expertise in creating mood, atmosphere and fantasy worlds with a direct evocation of cinema history. This leap occurred with her one-minute commercial for the reintroduction of the 1980s Panthére jewelry watch for Cartier (Liu 2017). Coppola takes her inspiration from the iconic 1980 film *American Gigolo*. *American Gigolo* presents the melodrama of a high-class male gigolo, Julian Kaye (Richard Gere) and his burgeoning relationship with a politician's wife (Lauren Hutton). Set against a murder investigation for which Julian is being framed, *American Gigolo* offers a compendium of early 80s fashion, style and culture. Coppola begins with a shot borrowed from *Gigolo*: a point-of-view shot of the bored Michelle sitting alone in a high-end restaurant/bar booth. Lauren Hutton has been replaced in the commercial by Australian Courtney Eaton. Coppola also inverts the focus so that she now tells the rich wife's tale, not the male gigolo's. The opening recreates, in careful detail, the upscale bar where the wife meets the gigolo for the first time. Traversing Beverly Hills in a Vintage Mercedes convertible afterwards (see Figure 5.6c), with sun filtered through the palm trees, Eaton ends up in the pool area of a mansion. She playfully kisses her boyfriend/husband (?) next to their pool's mansion. This leads to an intimate encounter in the bedroom and finally a night clubbing, dancing with friends.

The spot is scored to 'I Feel Love' by Donna Summer, invoking the queen of disco music from that era. The legacy continues with Eaton's friends being played by Donna Summer's real-life daughters, Brooklyn and Amanda Sudano. Evocation of a specific time, place and mood is augmented by this recreation of a cinematic text from the era, also heavily implicated in style, product and the good life. The commercial spot is able to place the 1980s luxury watch in the perfect environment located from film history. Coppola's choice to de-emphasize the watch compared to the affluent surroundings follows in the trajectory for luxury advertising; as Gillian Dyer explains it, 'The visual and verbal imagery evoke the status feelings associated with money, wealth, elegance, luxury and the public display of these things' (1982: 91). Coppola also blurs the lines between past and present, old and new in the appropriation of *American Gigolo* for this upscale advertising product.

The visual bursts in *The Virgin Suicides* yield moments of joy and enthusiasm, yet they occur in a context of loss and sadness. The boys are attempting to understand the tragedy of the Lisbon suicides through reviewing, for example, the happy moments from Cecilia's diary. I would suggest that this underlying poignancy extends to the Coppola commercials. Even with the joyous shots of abandonment, Coppola's 60 second commercials combine joy with a sense of melancholy, as in *The Virgin Suicides*. With Cartier and Daisy, evoking a time past (hippie-era 60s for Daisy, 80s for Cartier) gives each a nostalgic glow. With Marni for H&M, the structure of the heroine either recalling past fun or just dreaming it also suggests that the happiness lies in the past. This is underlined with Bryan Ferry intoning, 'The party's over, I'm so tired.' As with *The Virgin Suicides*, moments of fun and vitality (e.g., the car trip in the desert, swimming, the kiss) are bracketed by the serene and somber shots (e.g., waking up on the divan, gazing across the living room). Happiness is only fleeting in Coppola's visual aesthetic.

One Final Note: Transported to the World of Thorstein Veblen

Coppola's commercials invoke past worlds with the deep and textured imagery, but often they suggest much more. Many of the advertised products are classic examples of 'conspicuous consumption.' They suggest high quality, certainly, but also with a price tag that makes them unattainable for all but the richest 1% of our society. The Panthére Cartier watch, for instance, costs $8000. The commercials transport us more directly to Sofia's world. Assignments are justified on the level of personal relationships, such as her long-standing friendship with Marc Jacobs. In a break from the resolutely middle class world of *The Virgin Suicides*, Coppola shows an allegiance to Veblen-inspired life of fine goods, leisure-time, and family legacies. This tendency is reflected in many of her later feature films, most particularly *Marie Antoinette*, *Somewhere* and *The Bling Ring*. The benefits of commerce, wealth and tradition become a continuing theme for the director.

The shift from the middle class to the world of privilege is encapsulated nicely with the 2008 Louis Vuitton 'Core Values' ad shot by Annie Leibovitz. In what appears to be a movie location shoot, Father Francis gestures to Sofia who reclines on the barren plain. She looks up at her father, in awe or at least with great respect. Between them is a Vuitton bag stuffed with notebooks and files. The tagline reads 'Inside every story, there is a beautiful journey' (see Figure 5.7). Through the advertising image, Sofia Coppola's familial ties and legacy are made clear, all negotiated by the exotic location, the moviemaking background, and the high-end tote bag. For Sofia, the advertising imagery articulates her past, present and future: the emphasis on family and legacy, the commitment to a creative vision, and the aesthetic beauty of the product and, by extension, her filmmaking style. The advertising image, so crucial to *The Virgin Suicides* as a stylistic and thematic factor, becomes a way to return to Sofia Coppola. Interestingly, the earliest claims of elitism and privilege also come back with Sofia's invocation

Figure 5.7 Image from 2008 Louis Vuitton's Core Values campaign

of these rarified worlds with their beautiful products, images and surfaces. Advertising is a central force for Coppola, helping to shape her filmmaking style and reflect her own 'core values,' for better or worse.

Notes

1. As part of his review of *Marie Antoinette*, Nathan Lee (2006: 24–26) summarizes several of these claims against Coppola.
2. The exception to Coppola's typical style in her commercials can be seen in her Holiday Gap commercials from 2014. These 15 second spots are each based around an awkward or endearing anecdote from the holiday season. They are less focused on style and mise-en- scène and more focused on quirky 'gags' that quickly grab attention. Each ad ends with the tagline, 'You don't have to get them to get them Gap.' For a description of this four commercial series, see Toure (2014).
3. See 'Behind the Scenes of Marni H&M Commercial,' www.youtube.com/watch?v=A7x4pCMRVQw.

6   Sofia Coppola

The Virgin Suicides, Identity and Difference

Since the release of *The Virgin Suicides* in 1999, Coppola has directed five other feature films: *Lost in Translation* (2003), *Marie Antoinette* (2006), *Somewhere* (2010), *The Bling Ring* (2013) and *The Beguiled* (2017). These works have varied considerably in terms of critical and commercial reception, with *Lost in Translation* marking an early high water mark (including an Oscar for Coppola's screenplay). The project of building connections between Coppola's works is deceptive. On the downside, popular criticism, at times, seems to have crystallized around portraying Coppola as a film-maker focused on pretty visuals, beautiful people, and conspicuous consumption. Apart from *Lost in Translation*, the other Coppola films have been singled out for the beauty of the images at the expense of narrative. These criticisms do appear to have some traction, but I believe that they neglect the development of Coppola's filmmaking, aesthetically and narratively, over this period. Within the academy, however, Coppola's filmmaking, by individual film and across films, has received more consistent consideration and attention. Scholars such as Fiona Handyside (2017), Belinda Smaill (2013), and Todd Kennedy (2010) have assessed Coppola's oeuvre from multiple perspectives, especially through post-feminist readings. The startling debut of *The Virgin Suicides* did, indeed, promise a cinematic vision that is unique and singular.

To trace the connections, themes and storytelling devices through the films is a project substantially aided by invoking one key tenet of Coppola's filmmaking, the focus on identity formation. Certainly, the establishment of the adolescent—and then adult—identity is key to *The Virgin Suicides*. The difficulties with creating a stable identity echo throughout the subsequent films. To understand Coppola as an auteur is to address identity formation, the process through which identity can be formed and transformed in adolescence and beyond. In this chapter, I will trace how identity formation is so central to *The Virgin Suicides* and the subsequent Coppola films. While identity formation is crucial to theories of human development, Coppola's take reflects a specifically modern concern, the inability to create a coherent or stable identity in our (post) modern world. Identity is crucial to the diegetic world of Coppola's films, but it also has meaning far beyond. Viewed as a filmmaker, Coppola's own identity must be seen as shifting and developing. Part of the mainstream critical dialog over Coppola's artistry misses the ways through which her own artistic engagement has matured over time. The project then is two-fold in terms of identity formation: to understand the ways through which identity has structured the films, paying particular attention to works that feature adolescent or young adult characters, and to appreciate how Coppola's own artistic identity has been enriched across the works.

The Problem of Identity

Sociologists James E. Cote and Charles G. Levine sum up identity through three formations: social identity, personal identity, and ego identity. Each is differentiated through the particular set of attributes basing the identity. Social identity depends on identification with one or more groups, stressing the integration of the person with others. Personal identity, on the other hand, relies on individuation. Self-definition through appearance, speech and world view positions the individual as a unique member of society. Ego identity operates through agency, stressing the ability of the person to have a strong and valued image across a variety of social situations and across time (Cote and Levine 2016: 30). Cote and Levine make an important distinction about the efficacy of this model in our contemporary era. The traditional model of identity formation has become inadequate as the structures supporting individuals and groups have frayed over time. With social structures (family, work, church) less prominent than in the past, we are left with a 'longer period of youth' extending into adulthood. Markers of adulthood have been 'progressively destructured,' with the ability to establish stable and consistent identities increasingly difficult. In fact, Cote and Levine suggest that in the movement to the late modern era, social identities can be subsumed by the conspicuous consumption of goods and services (25). Personal identity becomes secondary to the social identity of consumption. The notion of a coherent and sustained identity is increasingly difficult to claim in our modern times.

Coppola's oeuvre reflects this disintegration of identity. *The Virgin Suicides* is a remarkable starting point for her exploration of the topic. Filtered through the boys' experiences and memories, the Lisbon sisters fail to develop individual identities. Excepting Lux, they are resigned to be objects of desire for the boys. The homogeneity of the sisters speaks to the boys' need to consider the girls largely for their sexual attractiveness. They are not permitted individual identities since that does not correspond to the way that the boys conceive of them.

Coppola's film speaks more directly to the splintered identities of the neighborhood boys. The film unfolds retrospectively from the perspective of neighborhood boys recounting the events from their Michigan adolescence twenty-five years ago. The narrative leads to the night of the suicides in which the boys are lured to the Lisbon household. They soon realize that their presumed road trip with the girls will be replaced by the 'suicide free-for-all.' Crucially, the motivation for the invitation that night is left unreconciled. Certainly the most likely reading is that the sisters wanted the boys to bear witness to the tragedy. The reason for this choice is left open: were the boys just convenient? Were they meant to be punished by the action? Were the girls hoping to implicate the boys in the actions in some way? By design, these questions are unanswered. The consequence scars the boys: they sift through the 'evidence' of the events over the years, trying to make sense of the events and, more specifically, their role in the tragedy.

From a psychological perspective, the experience of the boys falls into the territory of trauma. As Bessel A. Van Der Kolk and Onno Van Der Hart explain, vivid and scarring events during adolescence occupy a special place in terms of memory: 'Lack of proper integration of intensely emotionally arousing experiences into the memory system results in dissociation and the formation of traumatic memories' (1995: 163). Interestingly, the dissociation has a narrative component, or rather the lack of one: a consequence of the dissociation is the failure to assign the memory to a coherent narrative. Rather than reconcile the memory through a long or short narrative account, the dissociated events shift in the mind. Following on this pathway, the events associated with the traumatic incident become salient largely because of 'the quality of the experience and the feelings associated with it' (169). The impressionistic rendering in Coppola's film, as well as the detailed mise-en-scène, evocative music, and cinematography, all help to reflect the dissociated event linked to the adolescent trauma.

Ultimately, the identity of the boys/men is shaped negatively by the trauma they endured. The trauma creates their fixation on the event. With no answers forthcoming and the years clouding the events and the memories, the boys, now men, obsess on their adolescent trauma. The narrator recounts the neighborhood parents' response to the tragedy: returning soon after to their tennis games and to hosting a debutante party around the theme 'asphyxiation.' The implication is that the parents have a somewhat callous and unfeeling reaction to the mass suicide. While the boys salute the Lisbon home in the final scene, their own obsession remains despite their attempt at storytelling through the film. The film is set up as a recounting of the events leading up to the tragic night of the suicides. As dissociated events, however, the suicides and the events preceding fail to cohere narratively. In this way, Coppola's film actively reflects the psychological experience of trauma impacting identity. Narrative cannot contain the events. The result is a fixation on the traumatic events anchoring the men in their adolescence rather than allowing them to follow a natural path of maturation.

Impossible Identity in the Works of Sofia Coppola

Certainly the visual flourishes and signatures of Coppola are reflected across much of her work. These have received much attention in popular criticism.[1] The broken psyches and splintered identities in *The Virgin Suicides* play out just as vividly through subsequent films. Just as with the characters of *The Virgin Suicides*, the identities of other Coppola protagonists are derailed, with characters, either by their own volition or due to social structures, failing to establish a coherent, sustainable identity. The lack of a set identity can easily be seen as part of the postmodern condition, with identity mutable and fluid. Coppola's protagonists are, however, sketched in a more precise way. The identities are, for various reasons, 'on hold.' Although most of the characters are outside adolescence, the identities fix at a point where they are not fully engaged with daily lives, responsibilities or concerns. They are therefore not associated entirely with adulthood. As Cote and Levine suggest, in the late modern period, personal identity can become subsumed by 'image-oriented identity' predicated on accessing different social groups rather than building an individual identity (2016: 27). Coppola's characters play in this area of image orientation, sometimes with joy but often with pain and confusion.

Lost in Translation, *Marie Antoinette*, and *Somewhere* operate with protagonists whose identities are impacted by this dislocation. Coppola's May/November 'near romance' in *Lost in Translation* offers a paradigm for these broken characters. The lead characters—Yale philosophy graduate Charlotte (Scarlett Johansson) and has-been movie star Bob (Bill Murray)—meet in Tokyo at the Park Hyatt Hotel. The pair are jet-lagged, have difficulty negotiating the local culture, and, most tellingly, have ample free time to explore this new space. The cultural, temporal and spatial dislocation speaks to larger issues within the identities of these characters. Charlotte is accompanying her photographer husband on the trip simply since she has nothing else to do. Unsure how to translate her degree to employment, Charlotte feels more like a companion rather than a partner or wife. She is disconnected from her husband's activities (eschewing some of his professional/social obligations), and she seems to be a passive traveler (mostly preferring time alone in the hotel). Bob is all too aware of his lack of connection to others: his wife corresponds mainly through faxes and Fed Ex packages, his local 'handlers' fail to offer any guidance or support, and his career seems to have peaked about two decades earlier. Both characters have paused their identity (Charlotte until she can figure her next step into adulthood, Bob by accepting the whisky ads instead of pursuing legitimate acting jobs). Both are marked by a state of transience, in their identity and in their physicality. To her credit, Coppola does not offer easy answers for the pair. Whereas the genre of the romantic comedy might suggest that the pairing transforms the individual identities, Coppola only hints at any progress in the identity of her leads.

Coppola's next film also presents a protagonist traversing identity issues, largely without success or resolution. Kirsten Dunst, who played Lux Lisbon in *The Virgin Suicides*, is unveiled as Marie Antoinette, seen at first reclining on a divan, raising her eyebrows, and smiling mischievously at the camera. The film is structured around incongruities: an Austrian girl becoming French nobility; filming on locations of the actual events but using a 1980s new wave soundtrack predominantly; a cast with accents across the globe feigning to be French aristocracy (for instance, Coppola refers to actor Rip Torn in a commentary as 'the Texan King of France'). As with *Lost in Translation*, dislocation is central to the film. Marie is a young Austrian girl extricated to France for an arranged marriage. As with *The Virgin Suicides*, *Marie Antoinette* is sketched as a youth in crisis. The Lisbon sisters were ultimately powerless in their ability to shape their own world, leading to their own suicides. In the opening scenes, Marie Antoinette is presented by her mother as a solution to building bonds between two countries, Austria and France. The young Antoinette will become the Queen of France. Marie's agency in this matter is nil, and she is told to follow the advice of Ambassador Mercy closely. Her one companion, the little dog, Mops, is taken from her at the 'handover ceremony' between the two countries. Marie's entrance to the palace is shot primarily from her point-of-view. Her warm smiles are met overwhelmingly by indifference or hostility. Coppola offers her audience a young girl severed from her family, her culture, and her sources of comfort. Rather than use all of these as supports in developing an adult identity, Marie is placed into a permanent adolescence, with the consumption of luxury goods replacing all attempts at maturation. Critic Lesley Chow considers Marie Antoinette as typical of the Coppola heroines, young, adorned and abandoned: 'The Coppola ideal is a young girl trapped in fustiness: she can be an object of voyeurism without a trace of lewdness, and remain spiritually intact even when accessorized' (2007).

Coppola stresses the pomp and circumstance of the French royalty; Marie's morning dressing ceremony, for instance, is emphasized and becomes a motif throughout the film. Marie fails to develop, psychologically and intellectually, mainly because she is simply a vessel for these formalities. Even more, since the marriage is unconsummated for a long time, Marie becomes defined within the film largely in biological terms: she is blamed for not producing an heir. Ostracized by the French aristocracy, ridiculed by the courtiers, and isolated from her family, Marie takes refuge in the luxuries of fashion, food and leisure pastimes. Identity here is defined purely by the outer surfaces: fashion, style, ornamentation. Coppola regularly cuts to 'product shot,' to invoke an advertising term, of a dress detail, extravagant decoration, or sumptuous dessert. These direct shots of products replace the close-ups of the characters and their dramatic interactions. The appreciation of beautiful things rules over everything else in the film. If Marie Antoinette is able to assert any identity, it occurs through her fashion and style choices. Coppola suggests that her individuality derives from these style choices, even to the extent of shocking others in the palace. With this deflection though, Marie's identity also becomes fixed at her adolescence. Reflecting the modern situation of personal identity being subsumed by social identity, Marie Antoinette is portrayed as someone who is trapped in status and leisure at the expense of her personal development.

The social identity of consumption has stretched from Marie Antoinette to our contemporary times, the film seems to suggest. The negative impact on maturation and individuation has been intensified, and, of course, few today are able to assert their personalities solely through their high-end exclusive fashion and style choices. Interestingly, Coppola's later film *The Bling Ring* could be viewed as just that attempt at an adolescent defining oneself through the rarified levels of high-end consumption.

Four years after *Marie Antoinette*, *Somewhere* explores the issue of identity formation and the failure to develop in much more complicated terms. The film is a simple character study illustrating, over the course of a few weeks, the lives of movie action star Johnny Marco (Stephen Dorff) and his 11-year-old daughter, Cleo (Elle Fanning). At first glance, the film may appear to be a quiet observational drama, very episodic in structure. This reading fails to illuminate the real strengths of the film. Johnny is figured as a largely passive character. Despite his profession as actor, Johnny is most often watching the 'performance' of someone else: the pole-dancing twins in his hotel room, Cleo's ice skating routine, the spectacular Italian awards ceremony, and the serenading waiter at the Chateau Marmont. In this way, the film recalls Erving Goffman's dramaturgical model of identity formation (1969). Coppola presents her lead character as both the victim and product of performance: Johnny, the actor, is immobilized since everyone around Johnny is so anxious to perform for him. He is left as simply an empty shell of a character. Coppola pointedly creates situations that question the stable identity of the character. A lengthy scene shows a make-up and special effects team fitting Johnny for an old age mask. To fashion the make-up, the team takes molds a plastic mask onto Johnny. As it sets, the camera slowly zooms in on the actor, now rendered faceless and alone (see Figure 6.1). Similarly, at the movie press conference, the key question of 'Who is Johnny Marco?' is left unanswered by Johnny. In fact, Coppola waits a few beats before cutting to emphasize the lack of any answer. Throughout the film, Johnny is pursued by female admirers, all too willing to share an intimate encounter with him. Rather than engage emotionally, Johnny appears to go along with the sex just as a distraction. Indeed, in one late night encounter, Johnny, admittedly under the influence of pain medication, literally falls asleep while performing oral sex on his partner. The mode for Johnny is blank and open, almost as if an observer on his own life.

Identity formation is complicated substantially by placing the blank Johnny next to his young daughter Chloe. Chloe is presented as wise beyond her years. She instinctively takes care of her father: cooking for him, playing videogames with him, and simply being present with him in quiet times. Rather than a passive participant in life, Chloe is the one who plans activities even while part of her father's movie star life. When Johnny gets frantic thinking that their car is being followed by the paparazzi, Chloe calmly writes down the license plate to keep a record. Johnny is taken aback by her smart proactive decision making in the situation. Despite her youth, Chloe appears to be mature and centered in sharp contrast to her father. The role reversal, with daughter nurturing father, is a long-standing proposition. Johnny acquiesces to Cleo and her gentle warmth seems maternal in nature.

These roles are shattered in the final section of the film. As Johnny is driving Cleo to her summer camp, Cleo breaks down in tears. 'I don't know when Mom is coming back, and you're always gone,' she cries, more in

Figure 6.1 Johnny Marco (Stephen Dorff): the erasure of identity in *Somewhere* (2010)

resignation than in anger. This action inspires Johnny's hasty apology, muted by the sound of a helicopter, which is lost on Cleo. In the final act of the film, the stability of the identities has come undone. The fear of abandonment has made Cleo return, for the first time, to the vulnerability of being a young girl. Seeing this, Johnny is forced to face his own decisions privileging his party lifestyle over his young daughter. Both characters are placed in a situation where they must confront the artifice of their own identities: Cleo's maturity cannot hide that she still has the emotional needs of a young daughter; the disaffected Johnny must dissolve in face of his newly realized priorities in life. *Somewhere* does not sew up the identity issues in any easy manner. Coppola merely illustrates that positive change from Johnny is a distinct possibility.

Other films from Coppola also demonstrate issues in identity formation, albeit from a different perspective, namely the impact of poisonous social structures on the individual. Starting with *Lick the Star*, Coppola has also been interested in interrogating the ways through which social groups can dominate and obliterate an individual's personal identity. *The Bling Ring*'s teenage Hollywood gang is motivated to 'shop' from celebrity homes through a desire to fashion their identity close to the stars. They are presented as borderline social outcasts in their Valley high school. Largely neglected by their domestic families, the teens form their own family of friends dependent on partying, drugging and celebrity gossip. Rather than emulate fashion and style indirectly, social media and online infotainment give the friends access to the stars' homes and lives directly. Although theft is certainly part of their adventures, the teens spend time luxuriating in the stars' homes, trying on not just clothes but also the label of 'celebrity.' 'Let's go shopping' is the call-to-action for the teens, although 'shopping' is just a euphemism for stealing from celebrities. As with *Marie Antoinette*, identity is replaced with an adherence to extravagant and luxurious fashion and lifestyle items. Both Marie and the Bling Ring are unencumbered with the details of paying for their fashion choices. Social media allows the Bling Ring to telegraph their new looks, while the local nightclubs give them the chance to party right next to the celebrities.

The identities, of course, are paper thin, although surface counts for so much in our contemporary era. Several of the targets for the Bling Ring are celebrities, people like Paris Hilton, who are famous for being famous. Fame is presented as a matter of style and attitude. In this way, the teens from the Valley have just as much right to celebrity as anyone else. After the investigation and the arrest, the friendships between the gang members are revealed to be just as slight. At the end, each of the characters is betrayed by both their substitute family of mutual friends and by the larger celebrity culture. The friendships are based on simply holding a mirror to the images of the others, without any real emotional or psychological support at the basis. The sociopathic, and ultimately delusional, behavior of the teens is not a direct consequence of the social group. The behavior is, however, enabled and supported by the group of friends.

Apart from the poisonous social circle, *The Bling Ring* offers a fascinating take on the travails of youth identity formation in our contemporary era. The social group influences are, of course, paramount, partly due to the failure of parents and other authority figures. Parents are either absent or depicted as trying too hard to be friends with their children. Laurie (Leslie Mann) is the best example of this latter tendency. She homeschools her daughters who pay almost no attention to the curricular activities, such as creating a 'vision board' of positive attributes of stars like Angelina Jolie. Laurie has no control over their curfew and takes at face value the wild lies and schemes presented to her. The implication is that the parents offer neither real guidance nor role models for their teens. Social media and celebrity infotainment are much more potent as means to fabricate an identity. As Delphine Letort explains, identity for these characters is linked inextricably to a kind of generic female celebrity image: 'The physical resemblance between the girls of the Bling Ring also testifies to the pervasive influence of stereotypical celebrities, who embody a type of femininity characterized by long hair, high-heeled shoes, sunglasses, slim trousers, etc.' (2016: 313).

The impact of the group on identity dominates the film as a structuring device. Coppola also, however, presents a very specific instance of identity formation in *The Bling Ring*. Although largely an ensemble film, the young gay male teen Marc (Israel Broussard) arguably receives a more careful treatment than the others. Unlike the other members of the group, Marc is depicted as someone who is desperately looking for his place in society. His identity is firmly tied up with interpersonal acceptance; he needs to be accepted by a group of his peers. Coppola saw Marc as being her entry point to the story, and she was attracted by the notion of an identity changing: 'I thought he was really the most sympathetic one—you could understand how he could have gotten caught up in this group and why he wanted to be a part of it. I remembered being that age and, you know, you do things you wouldn't do as an adult, because you want the excitement of feeling like you're part of something' (quoted in Gevinson 2013).

As with many young gay people, Marc is looking for his 'family of choice' among those who can accept him and his sexuality. In an early scene, Marc explains that he has always been self-conscious since he perceived that he wasn't as good looking as other people. This kind of self-devaluation has been characteristic of the gay developmental struggle; as Ritch Savin-Williams and Richard Rodriguez explain, this process arises from 'the institutional, interpersonal and psychological processes

attached to being a member of a socially stigmatized or oppressed group'
(1993: 89). Starting at Indian Hills High School after being expelled from
his last school, Marc is befriended by Rebecca (Katie Chang) who quickly
indoctrinates him to high-end theft and grifting (see Figure 6.2). Although
Rebecca seems largely immune to building an emotional connection, Marc
is clearly attached to her. He explains his relationship in this manner: 'I
loved her. I really did. She was the first person I felt was like a best friend.
I loved her like a sister. That's what made it so hard.' Throughout the bur-
glaries, Marc is the most cautious, suggesting when to leave and identifying risks. As a result, he is often the target of derision by the others. In the
most vivid example of this, he is tormented with a gun by one of the gang
during a robbery. Apart from the pair of hot pink high heels he steals from
Paris Hilton, Marc's pleasure from consumption is largely second-hand: he
offers styling advice for the girls while they are wearing the stolen clothes.
Coppola paints Marc as motivated more by the social acceptance offered
by the gang. The robberies and fame are seen as being secondary pleasures
for the boy. Coppola concludes with a lengthy and largely silent scene of
Marc entering the county jail bus on route to his imprisonment. His group
affiliation has shifted from his chic female friends to a set of much older,
hardened male prisoners. Coppola's grim coda to Marc's story positions
the even greater difficult of being LGBTQ and young in terms of identity
formation.

Figure 6.2 Rebecca (Katie Chang) and Marc (Israel Broussard): social media as
identity in *The Bling Ring* (2013)

The toxic social circle recurs in Coppola's adaptation of Thomas Cullinan's novel, *The Beguiled*. Filmed previously in 1971 by Don Siegel, Coppola's 2017 film of the Civil War story details a wounded Northern soldier, Corporal McBurney (Colin Farrell) taken in by a Southern girls' school. The headmistress, Miss Martha (Nicole Kidman), attempts to set the parameters of McBurney's interactions with the school. Flirtations with teacher Edwina (Kirsten Dunst) and student Alicia (Elle Fanning) lead in a different direction, however. The demure inhabitants of Miss Martha's school eventually become associated with amputation and even homicide. The film is structured around the tension between the social identity and the personal identity of each character. While each character must play their social roles (headmistress, teacher, student), their personal desires increasingly play against their social responsibilities. The presence of the male figure in the school ignites not just sexual attraction, but also a breakdown of the social roles. Miss Martha's move to amputate the soldier's leg seems like retribution for Alicia's dalliance with McBurney and Edwina's developing personal relationship with the soldier. As the other women have pursued their attraction for McBurney, Miss Martha's ability to maintain control and order over the school is more tenuous. Social order is threatened by personal identity. The identity of each female character becomes splintered as the strain between the personal and social becomes unbearable. By the end, the individual identities have been muted once again in service of the social roles. Each female character passively assumes their assigned role as they wait for the soldiers to claim McBurney's dead body.

Auteur Identity Formation

Working through the complexities of identity is crucial to the Coppola cinema, and it may well be for the filmmaker herself. Only age 28 during the production of *The Virgin Suicides*, Coppola's identity to date had been marked, at points, by significant personal tragedy and professional humiliation. As Andrew Barnaby suggests, summarizing prior psychoanalytic work on the impact of trauma on identity, 'Trauma renders experience inaccessible to conscious thought' (2012: 119). Coppola's personal history intersects with several of the themes in *The Virgin Suicides*: victimization, social alienation, and the passivity of having others define you. While these themes are engaged with directly in *The Virgin Suicides*, Coppola's subsequent films work through the issues via the filter of her personal history. As a result, the post-*Suicides* films echo themes of her debut film, but they also present an increasingly personal dialog with Coppola herself. In this way, the films evidence a growth and evolution which sometimes goes unnoticed by popular and academic critics.

In assessing the impact of her filmmaking, academic critics tend to engage with feminism as the label to define Coppola's cinema.[2] Fiona Handyside, for example, characterizes Coppola through her ability to 'carve out new spaces of female subjectivity that embrace rather than reject femininity.' This embrace of femininity is manifested through 'repeated motifs of sex, travel, shopping and makeovers as empowerment' (2017: 5). Rather than argue for a post-feminist perspective, Belinda Smaill makes the case for the Coppola oeuvre in terms of a traditional feminist intervention. Drawing on Patrice Petro's theories of boredom, repetition and renewal in women's lives, Smaill sees these structures as crucial to Coppola's filmmaking: 'The notion of duration, repetition and active waiting are unmistakable elements of Coppola's oeuvre. Looking at her cinema in this way opens a door to viewing Coppola's practice as not outside, but entrenched in a continuum of women's cultural production' (2013: 157). Todd Kennedy also sees the potential for Coppola's cinema as a kind of filmmaking outside the patriarchal norm. In fact, Kennedy invokes Claire Johnston's notion of women's cinema as counter-cinema to describe Coppola's filmmaking. Coppola's counter-cinema is manifested through figuring a new spectatorial position:

> Her films repeatedly ask the audience to associate themselves with a feminine point of view as, in absence of the ability to depict "real" women, Coppola asks her audience to become real women: to be gazed upon, objectified, and, even more importantly, aware of their complicit participation in this objectification.
>
> (2010: 56)

Kennedy assigns the split critical reaction over Coppola to this new feminine auteurship. The films present the viewer with an unexpected means into their stories and characters, threatening the norms of conventional Hollywood storytelling.

Locating Coppola's auteurism in *The Virgin Suicides* is complicated since much of the film's power is derived from Coppola's storytelling, visual and aural, of the Eugenides source material. Certainly, some of the most striking techniques and devices—the detailed mise-en-scène, the moments of reverie, and the juxtaposition of music/image—in *The Virgin Suicides* echo throughout the subsequent films. Other key aspects of Coppola's biography—gifted, creative, privileged, a lover of fine aesthetics—shine through much more strongly in the later films. In conjunction with the 'stand-in' young female heroines (Scarlett Johansson in *Lost in Translation*, Kirsten Dunst in *Marie Antoinette*), critics have tended to slip between aspects of Sofia Coppola's image and the heroines of the films. Belinda Smaill refers to the focus on surfaces within the work as defining it as 'unworthy or questionable art cinema, one that does not infuse the minimalism of its plots and carefully composed imagery with adequate relevance and complexity' (2013: 151). This critique disregards the development in the works and the deepening of the style across the films.

This evolution can be seen through the ways in which Coppola uses storytelling techniques to engage the issues of identity formation so crucial to her films. In *The Virgin Suicides*, using the perspective of the plural male narrator recalling events from a quarter of a century ago allows Coppola to present distorted events, characters and incidents in line with the failing point-of-view. With *Lost in Translation*, the key elements of spatial, temporal and cultural dislocation inspire the narrative events and highlight the broken identities of the two leads. *Marie Antoinette* evidences a greater self-consciousness in technique: the direct address to the camera, the purposefully anachronistic flourishes, and, of course, the absolute fascination with conspicuous consumption. The last plays out through the costuming, hair/make-up, food, ornamentation, and, of course, the real locations in Versailles. Whereas the narration in *The Virgin Suicides* and the structural parameters of *Lost in Translation* center each film's investigation of identity, the emphasis on surfaces in *Marie Antoinette*, at first glance, might appear to be a step backwards. As Nathan Lee commented on the film in *Film Comment*, 'Sensibility is everything in Coppola. To accuse her of lacking ideas presumes she has any interest in them' (2006: 25). Keep in mind though that moments of quiet contemplation are included throughout the film giving the viewer a picture of Marie's inner state and her melancholy. Popular critics glossed over these moments to focus on the extravagant visual design instead. Privileging the look of the film over character and storyline became the main issue leveled against Coppola as a filmmaker.

Initially, *Somewhere* may appear to be a chamber piece like *Lost in Translation*: the story of two characters involved in an intimate emotional relationship. This reading elides the movement forward by Coppola as a filmmaker. *Lost in Translation* is marked by a series of near 'encounters' which culminate in the secret whisper from Bob to Charlotte. *Somewhere* presents a more complex relationship, this time between father Johnny Marco and daughter Cleo. Unlike the frantic energy and overwhelming mise-en-scène of *Marie Antoinette*, the film is told in simple terms: quotidian actions featured in long takes, often at a distance; all shot on location at the Chateau Marmont and other locations in Los Angeles. The film's action is anecdotal, although Coppola is clear in setting the time frame and enough narrative turning points to give the film a coherent structure.

Rather than shy away from the emotional development of the characters, Coppola commits to following Johnny's breakdown and existential crisis.

Apparently inspired by Cleo crying over her absent parents, the final chapters of the film recount Johnny undergoing a personal crisis. His apology ('Cleo, sorry I haven't been around') is mostly lost in the noise of the nearby helicopter. Johnny attempts, without success, to bond with a friend over the phone. Coppola continues with long-running shots leading to the final shot of Johnny abandoning his car on the side of the road. The implication is that he will be reassessing his priorities given his time with Cleo and the realization of his empty daily life. Delicately, Coppola suggests a transformation without specifying the particular 'next steps' for Johnny. As she comments on *Somewhere*'s conclusion, 'I like endings where you get to think about what happens but you give an indication. To me it's frustrating when there's *no* indication' (quoted in Rapold 2010: 33). Coppola reaches her conclusion by joining the precise cinematic techniques with the realistic, incremental narrative. The maturity of the film comes from the unexpected emotional depth when the possibility for identity and growth is addressed directly (rather than being ignored or displaced in the previous Coppola films).

Contrary to much popular criticism, *Somewhere* illustrates that Coppola has an emotional valence to her work. In this way, the claims of vagueness evident in *Lost in Translation* and *Marie Antoinette* cannot be applied to her portrait of an actor's gentle and tenuous relationship with his daughter. *The Virgin Suicides* was so startling for presenting a new director whose command of the cinematic language perfectly matched the weighty themes of Jeffrey Eugenides' narrative. The subsequent films have demonstrated Coppola's ability to hone her storytelling abilities. The techniques illustrate Coppola's willingness to experiment with time, space and conventional expectations from narrative. All of these devices though are in aid of understanding character and aligning the viewer with an observational reality for her characters. In this way, Coppola is, indeed, presenting a 'counter-cinema' extending and morphing the outlines of conventional Hollywood storytelling.

The Legacy of *The Virgin Suicides*

The Lisbon sisters will remain a mystery to the neighborhood boys despite all their efforts to uncover the reasons behind the tragedy. The enigma of the girls is largely one of identity: the teen boys have no idea how to engage with and connect to the girls. They also fail to understand the girls' concerns in any substantive way. The mystery of identity becomes a trauma for the boys who are forever stuck in the 1970s Michigan suburbs of their minds. Linked to the narrative through personal tragedy and public humiliation, director Sofia Coppola transformed the Eugenides narrative into a compelling cinematic experience. Her ability to orchestrate sound and image in a context far apart from the usual Hollywood norms marked her feature debut. Youth in peril—under siege by social structures, family, school, illness and other forces—has been a staple in Hollywood since *Rebel Without a Cause* (Nicholas Ray, 1955). Coppola offers her viewers a wide variety of youths—from the brash teen boys to the suicidal sisters—and paints their reality with depth and texture through her cinematic devices (e.g., the reveries, the use of music, the shifts in perspective and tone). Identity and cinematic artistry go hand-in-hand through these depictions of youth in distress. And even though Coppola's aesthetic approach to *The Virgin Suicides* makes for a film that does not target, at least consciously, youth audiences, it nonetheless certainly engages with key issues relevant to this group, and therefore remains a film *about* youth, to paraphrase Jon Lewis (1992: 2).

The divided critical reaction to Coppola after *The Virgin Suicides* reflects the difficulties with pinning down Coppola as an auteur. The immediate follow-up, *Lost in Translation*, is critically lauded and wins a Best Original Screenplay Oscar for Coppola; *Marie Antoinette* generates boos at its Cannes premiere and largely underwhelms both viewers and critics; *Somewhere* is ignored and barely released; *The Bling Ring* and *The Beguiled* receive mixed reviews but disappoint at the box office. While all the films are extremely carefully crafted, the storytelling mechanisms shift film to film. The anachronistic displays and music videos of *Marie Antoinette* exist in a much different directorial universe than the quiet observational cinema of *Somewhere* or *The Beguiled*. The energetic and richly textured luxury good commercials also signal another completely different direction for understanding Coppola as a director. At best, one must say that these diverse styles are not reconciled. Pinpointing the identity of the auteur is just as difficult as understanding the complex motivations and drives of the lead characters within the Coppola films. The traits of Coppola's auteurism have evolved over time. Consistently though the post-*Virgin Suicides* films address the concept of identity in flux or in process through a battery of cinematic techniques manipulating time, space and narrative. These techniques are largely outside conventional genres and they do extend the vocabulary of cinematic storytelling. With their deep engagement with the frailties of human nature, Coppola's work feels better labelled as humanist storytelling rather than feminist cinema or post-feminist cinema. For Coppola, the quiet observation of the human condition, in both positive and negative terms, began with *The Virgin Suicides* and continues to this day.

Notes

1. See, for examples, the brief but illuminating visual analyzes in the videos 'The BFI Guide on How to Make a Sofia Coppola Film' and 'Color by Numbers:

The Films of Sofia Coppola' (Fandor). Both stress the use of color and natural light as structuring elements, although the Fandor video points out that there are relatively few pastels in the Coppola films. Instead the films are dominated by a constrained set of colors with minor variations from each other. See BFI (2017) 'The BFI Guide on How to Make a Sofia Coppola Film,' YouTube, online 12 July, www.youtube.com/watch?v=y7Jqpxy0CNg and Fandor (2017) 'Color by Numbers: The Films of Sofia Coppola,' YouTube, online, 19 June, www.youtube.com/watch?v=djN8YllY4cs.

2. It should be noted that Christina Lane and Nicole Richter present a compelling analysis of the larger industrial factors at play in Sofia Coppola's authorship. As they describe Coppola's method, 'The director has always shown skill in cultivating hybrid production and distribution arrangements with an eye toward the global market' (2011: 191).

Bibliography

Aaron, M. (2014) 'Cinema and Suicide: Necromanticism, Dead-Alreadyness, and the Logic of the Vanishing Point,' *Cinema Journal*, 53.2, Winter, pp. 71–92.

Adams, G., Gullotta, T. and Montemayor, R. (eds) (1992) *Adolescent Identity Formation*, Newbury Park: Sage Publications.

Aftab, K. (2010) 'Francis Ford Coppola—It's All About the Family Business,' *The Independent*, online, 10 June, www.independent.co.uk/arts-entertainment/films/features/francis-ford-coppola-its-all-about-the-family-business-1996839.html.

Anderson, T. (2008) 'As If History Was Merely a Record: The Pathology of Nostalgia and the Figure of the Recording in Contemporary Popular Cinema,' *Music, Sound and the Moving Image*, 2.1, Spring, pp. 51–76.

Anderson, T. (2013) 'Lost in Transition: Popular Music, Adolescence and the Melodramatic Mode of Sofia Coppola,' in Ashby, A. (ed) *Popular Music and the Post-MTV Auteur: Visionary Filmmakers After MTV*, Oxford: Oxford University Press, pp. 63–83.

Angley, N. (2015) 'Sexist Ads in "the Seventies",' *CNN*, online, 22 July, http://edition.cnn.com/2015/07/22/living/seventies-sexist-ads/.

Anon (1986) 'Francis Coppola's Son Killed in Motorboating Accident,' *The New York Times*, online, 28 May, www.nytimes.com/1986/05/28/obituaries/francis-coppola-s-son-killed-in-a-motorboating-accident.html.

Anon (2012) 'French Electronic Music: A History of Global Success,' *France in the United States*, online, 24 October, https://franceintheus.org/spip.php?article4012.

Anon (2017) '7 Must-Haves for a Quintessential Sofia Coppola Film,' *Focus Features*, online, 12 May, www.focusfeatures.com/article/celebrating_happy-birthday-sofia-coppola.

Attali, J. (1985) *Noise: The Political Economy of Music*, Minneapolis: University of Minnesota Press.

Backman Rogers, A. (2012) 'Ephemeral Bodies and Threshold Creatures: The Crisis of the Adolescent Rite of Passage in Sofia Coppola's *The Virgin Suicides* and Gus Van Sant's *Elephant*,' *European Journal of Media Studies*, 1.1, pp. 148–168.

Bahiana, A. M. (2017) 'Francis Ford Coppola: An Offer He Couldn't Refuse,' *Scraps from the Loft*, online, 2 January, http://scrapsfromtheloft.com/2017/01/02/francis-ford-coppola-an-offer-he-couldnt-refuse/.

Balk, D., Cavuoti, C. and Smith, A. M. (2017) 'Adolescent Sibling Loss,' in Marshall, B. and Winokeur, H. (eds) *Sibling Loss Across the Lifespan: Research, Practice and Personal Stories*, New York: Routledge, pp. 49–57.

Barnaby, A. (2012) 'Coming Too Late: Freud, Belatedness, and Existential Trauma,' *SubStance*, 41.2, pp. 119–138.

Bennett, J. (1961) 'The Essences of Being,' *The Hudson Review*, 14.3, Autumn, pp. 432–436.

Benning, S. and Smith, G. (1998) 'Toy Stories,' *Film Comment*, 34.6, November, pp. 28–33.

Blasberg, D. (2014) 'Mark and Sofia: The Dreamy Team,' *Harper's Bazaar*, online, 13 August, www.harpersbazaar.com/fashion/designers/a3169/marc-jacobs-sofia-coppola-0914/.

Bordwell, D. (1985) *Narration in the Fiction Film*, Madison: University of Wisconsin Press.

Campbell, P., Connell, C. and Beegle, A. (2007) 'Adolescents' Expressed Meanings of Music in and Out of School,' *Journal of Research in Music Education*, 55.3, Autumn, pp. 220–236.

Carson, M., Lewis, T. and Shaw, S. (2015) *Girls Rock: Fifty Years of Women Making Music*, Lexington: University of Kentucky Press.

Chow, L. (2007) 'Fashion and Dunst: The Substance of *Marie Antoinette*,' *Bright Lights Film Journal*, online, 1 May, http://brightlightsfilm.com/fashion-dunst-substance-marie-antoinette/#.WmjusDdOnIU.

Colman, F. (2005) 'Hit Me Harder: The Transversality of Becoming Adolescent,' *Women: A Cultural Review*, 16.3, pp. 356–371.

Coppola, E. (1979) *Notes*, New York: Simon and Schuster.

Coppola, E. (2008) *Notes on a Life*, New York: Applause Books.

Cote, J. (2000) *Arrested Adulthood: The Changing Nature of Identity and Maturity in the Late-Modern World*, New York: New York University Press.

Cote, J. and Levine, C. (2016) *Identity Formation, Youth and Development*, New York: Psychology Press.

Cross, G. (2002) 'Valves of Desire: A Historian's Perspective on Parents, Children, and Marketing,' *Journal of Consumer Research*, 29.3, pp. 441–447.

Denney, J. and Teachman, J. (2010) 'Family and Household Formations and Suicide in the United States,' *Journal of Marriage and Family*, 72.1, pp. 202–213.

Durkheim, E. (2006) *On Suicide*, London: Penguin Classics.

Dyer, G. (1982) *Advertising as Communication*, London: Methuen.

Dyer, R. (1979) *Stars*, London: British Film Institute.

Eugenides, J. (1993) *The Virgin Suicides*, New York: Picador.

Ewens, H. (2016) 'What Marie Antoinette Taught Me about Being a Teenage Girl,' *Vice*, online, 5 July, www.vice.com/en_us/article/qbn897/the-film-that-made-me-marie-antoinette-sofia-coppola.

Frank, T. (1997) *The Conquest of Cool: Business Culture, Counterculture and the Rise of Hip Consumerism*, Chicago: University of Chicago Press.

Frith, S. (1984) 'Rock and the Politics of Memory,' *Social Text*, 9/10, Spring–Summer, pp. 59–69.

Frith, S. (2007) *Taking Popular Music Seriously*, Aldershot: Ashgate.

Garber, M. (2015) '"You've Come a Long Way, Baby": The Lag Between Advertising and Feminism,' *The Atlantic*, online, 15 June, www.theatlantic.com/entertainment/archive/2015/06/advertising-1970s-womens-movement/395897/.

Gerosa, M. (1991) 'Goddaughter,' *Entertainment Weekly*, 25 January, pp. 12–17.

Gevinson, T. (2013) 'Girls with Power and Mystique: An Interview with Sofia Coppola,' *Rookiemag*, online, 17 June, www.rookiemag.com/2013/06/sofia-coppola-interview/.

Goffman, E. (1969) *The Presentation of Self in Everyday Life*, New York: Doubleday.

Handyside, F. (2017) *Sofia Coppola: A Cinema of Girlhood*, London: I.B. Taurus.

Harrington, J. (2006) 'Air: *The Virgin Suicides* (2000),' in Dimery, R. (ed) *1001 Albums You Must Hear Before You Die*, New York: Universe.

Hine, T. (2007) *The Great Funk*, New York: Farrar, Strauss and Giroux.

Jackson, D. (2016) 'Answering the Call,' in Casper, M. and Werteimer, E. (eds) *Critical Trauma Studies: Understanding Violence, Conflict and Memory in Everyday Life*, New York: NYU Press, pp. 205–226.

James, D. E. (1989) *Allegories of Cinema: American Film in the Sixties*, Princeton: Princeton University Press.

Jones, D. (2015) 'What You Didn't Know About the Virgin Suicides Soundtrack,' *Dazed*, online, 22 June, www.dazeddigital.com/music/article/25159/1/what-you-didn-t-know-about-the-virgin-suicides-soundtrack.

Kael, P. (2017) '*The Godfather Part III* (1990): Review by Pauline Kael,' *Scraps From the Loft*, online, 18 August, http://scrapsfromtheloft.com/2017/08/18/godfather-part-iii-1990-review-pauline-kael/.

Keightley, K. (1996) '"Turn It Down!" She Shrieked: Gender, Domestic Space, and High Fidelity, 1948–1959,' *Popular Music*, 15.2, pp. 149–177.

Keightley, K. (2008) 'Music for Middlebrows: Defining the Easy Listening,' *American Music*, 26.3, pp. 309–335.

Kennedy, T. (2010) 'Off with Hollywood's Head: Sofia Coppola as Feminine Auteur,' *Film Criticism*, 35.1, Fall, pp. 37–59.

Klein, M. (1940) 'Mourning and Its Relation to Manic-Depressive States,' *The International Journal of Psychoanalysis*, 21, pp. 125–153.

Koestenbaum, W. (2011) *Humiliation*, New York: Picador.

Lane, C. (2005) 'Just Another Girl Outside the Neo-Indie,' in Holmlund, C. and Wyatt, J. (eds) *Contemporary American Independent Cinema: From the Margins to the Mainstream*, New York: Routledge, pp. 193–209.

Lane, C. and Richter, N. (2011) 'The Feminist Poetics of Sofia Coppola: Spectacle and Self-Consciousness in *Marie Antoinette* (2006),' in Radner, H. and Stringer, R. (eds) *Feminism at the Movies: Understanding Gender in Contemporary Popular Cinema*, New York: Routledge, pp. 189–202.

Lee, N. (2006) 'Pretty Vacant,' *Film Comment*, 42.5, September/October, pp. 24–26.

Letort, D. (2016) 'The Cultural Capital of Sofia Coppola's *The Bling Ring* (2013): Branding Feminine Celebrity in Los Angeles,' *Celebrity Studies*, 7.3, pp. 309–322.

Lewis, J. (1992) *The Road to Romance and Ruin: Teen Films and Youth Culture*, New York: Routledge.

Lewis, J. (1995) *Whom God Wishes to Destroy: Francis Coppola and the New Hollywood*, Durham: Duke University Press.

Lindsay, R. (2004) 'Promises to Keep,' in Phillips, G. D. and Hill, R. (eds) *Francis Ford Coppola: Interviews*, Jackson: University Press of Mississippi, pp. 132–142.

Liu, M. (2017) 'Sofia Coppola Directs for Cartier,' *The New York Times*, online, 17 May, www.nytimes.com/2017/05/17/fashion/jewelry-cartier-panthere-sofia-coppola.html?_r=0.

Lynn, S. (2008) *Texts and Contexts: Writing About Literature With Critical Theory*, New York: Pearson Longman.

McCall, C. (2012) 'The Sexualization of Women and Girls,' *Psychology Today*, online, 4 March, www.psychologytoday.com/blog/overcoming-child-abuse/201203/the-sexualization-women-and-girls.

McFerran, K. (2010) *Adolescents, Music and Music Therapy*, London: Jessica Kingsley Publishers.

Montgomery, K. (1989) *Target: Prime Time: Advocacy Groups and the Struggle Over Entertainment Television*, New York: Oxford University Press.

Mulvey, L. (1975) 'Visual Pleasure and Narrative Cinema,' *Screen*, 16.3, October, pp. 6–18.

Myers, O. (2013) 'Jeffrey Eugenides' *Virgin Suicides*,' *Dazed*, online, 6 August, www.dazeddigital.com/artsandculture/article/16814/1/jeffrey-eugenides-virgin-suicides.

Naremore, J. (1990) 'Authorship and the Cultural Politics of Film Criticism,' *Film Quarterly*, 44.1, Autumn, pp. 14–23.

Newman, M. Z. (2011) *Indie: An American Film Culture*, New York: Columbia University Press.

Osgerby, B. (2008) 'Understanding the "Jackpot Market": Media, Marketing and the Rise of the American Teenager,' in Jamieson, P. and Romer, D. (eds) *The Changing Portrayal of Adolescence in the Media Since 1950*, New York: Oxford University Press, pp. 27–58.

Phillips, G. D. and Hill, R. (2004) *Francis Ford Coppola: Interviews*, Jackson: University Press of Mississippi, p. 140.

Pollock, G. (1989) 'The Mourning Process, the Creative Process and the Creation,' in Dietrich, D. and Shabad, P. (eds) *The Problem of Loss and Mourning: Psychoanalytic Perspectives*, Madison: International Universities Press, pp. 27–60.

Portner, J. (2001) *One in Thirteen: The Silent Epidemic of Teen Suicide*, Beltsville: Robins Lane Press.

Pruitt, L. (2013) *Youth Peacebuilding: Music, Gender and Chance*, Albany: SUNY Press.

Rachel, T. C. (2015) 'Q&A: Air's Jean-Benoît Dunckel on the Future of the Band, Working With Sofia Coppola, and Inspiring the Name "Stereogum",' *Stereogum*, online, 14 August, www.stereogum.com/1823047/qa-airs-jean-benoit-dunckel-on-the-future-of-the-band-working-with-sofia-coppola-and-inspiring-the-name-stereogum/franchises/interview/.

Ramey, S. (2015) *The Sister Pact*, Naperville: Sourcebooks Fire.

Rapold, N. (2010) 'Living in the Limelight,' *Film Comment*, 46.6, November/December, pp. 30–33.

Reichardt, K. and Haynes, T. (1995) 'Interview,' *BOMB*, 53, Fall, pp. 11–12 and 14–15.

Rich, B. R. (1992) 'New Queer Cinema,' *Sight & Sound*, 2.5, September, pp. 30–34.

Roeder, J. D. (1999) 'Consumer Socialization of Children: A Retrospective Look at Twenty-Five Years of Research,' *Journal of Consumer Research*, 26.3, pp. 183–213.

Roeg, N. (2013) *The World Is Ever Changing*, London: Faber and Faber.

Rosenbaum, J. (1989) 'Review of *New York Stories*,' *The Chicago Reader*, online, 3 March, www.jonathanrosenbaum.net/1989/03/three-of-a-kind/.

Sajbel, M. (1989) 'Daughter Dearest,' *Women's Wear Daily*, 1 March.

Savin-Williams, R. and Rodriguez, R. (1993) 'A Developmental, Clinical Perspective on Lesbian, Gay Male and Bisexual Youths,' in Gullotta, T., Adams, G. and Montemayor, R. (eds) *Adolescent Sexuality*, Newbury Park: Sage Publications, pp. 77–101.

Schiff, J. (2006) 'A Conversation with Jeffrey Eugenides,' *The Missouri Review*, 29.3, Fall, pp. 100–119.

Schneider, K. and Barich Schneider, S. (1979) 'Trends in Sex Roles in Television Commercials,' *Journal of Marketing*, 42, Summer, pp. 79–84.

Scott, A. O. (2000) 'Evanescent Trees and Sisters in an Enchanted 1970's Suburb,' *The New York Times*, online, 21 April, www.nytimes.com/2000/04/21/movies/film-review-evanescent-trees-and-sisters-in-an-enchanted-1970-s-suburb.html.

Shaffer, M. (2017) 'Interview with Eleanor Coppola: Director of "Paris Can Wait",' *Vague Visages*, online, 26 May, https://vaguevisages.com/2017/05/26/interview-eleanor-coppola-director-paris-can-wait/.

Shostak, D. (2009) '"A Story We Could Live With": Narrative Voice, the Reader and Jeffrey Eugenides's *The Virgin Suicides*,' *Modern Fiction Studies*, 55.4, Winter, pp. 808–832.

Shostak, D. (2013) '"Impossible Narrative Voices": Sofia Coppola's Adaptation of Jeffrey Eugenides's *The Virgin Suicides*,' *Interdisciplinary Literary Studies*, 15.2, pp. 180–202.

Simpson, M. (1981) 'Does She or Doesn't She? Revisited: The Calvin Klein Jeans Ads,' *ETC: A Review of General Semantics*, 38.4, Winter, pp. 390–400.

Smaill, B. (2013) 'Sofia Coppola: Reading the Director,' *Feminist Media Studies*, 13.1, pp. 148–162.

Smith, N. (2004) 'And the Beat Goes On: An Introduction to French Techno Culture,' *The French Review*, 77.4, pp. 730–741.

Soley, L. and Kurzbard, G. (1986) 'Sex in Advertising: A Comparison of 1964 and 1984 Magazine Advertisements,' *Journal of Advertising*, 15.3, pp. 46–64.

Steele, J. and Brown, J. (1995) 'Adolescent Room Culture: Studying Media in the Context of Everyday Life,' *Journal of Youth and Adolescence*, 24.5, pp. 551–576.

Stilwell, R. (2006) 'Vinyl Communion: The Record as Ritual Object in Girls' Rites of Passage Films,' in Powrie, P. and Stilwell, R. (eds) *Changing Tunes: Issues in Music and Film*, Aldershot: Ashgate Press, pp. 152–166.

Toure, M. (2014) 'Sofia Coppola Directs Gap's Holiday Ads from Wieden & Kennedy,' *Advertising Age*, online, 29 October, http://adage.com/article/advertising/watch-gap-s-sofia-coppola-directed-holiday-ads/295644/.

Usuda, K. (2008) 'The Voice of Marianne Faithfull on Sofia Coppola's *Marie Antoinette*,' *Cineaction*, 75, Winter, pp. 54–57.

Van Der Kolk, B. and Van Der Hart, O. (1995) 'The Intrusive Past: The Flexibility of Memory and the Engraving of Trauma,' in Caruth, C. (ed) *Trauma: Explorations in Memory*, Baltimore: The Johns Hopkins Press, pp. 158–182.

Weller, S. (2008) *Girls Like Us: Carole King, Joni Mitchell, Carly Simon—and the Journey of a Generation*, New York: Washington Square Press.

Williamson, J. (1978) *Decoding Advertisements: Ideology and Meaning in Advertising*, London: Marion Boyars.

Wojcik Robertson, P. (2001) 'The Girl and the Phonograph; or the Vamp and the Machine,' in Wojcik Robertson, P. and Knight, A. (eds) *Soundtrack Available: Essays on Film and Popular Music*, Durham: Duke University Press, pp. 433–454.

Woodhead, H. (2017) 'What Sofia Coppola's Films Taught Me about Being a Teenage Girl,' *Little White Lies*, online, 24 June, http://lwlies.com/articles/sofia-coppola-films-the-virgin-suicides-teenage-girl/.

Index